CHILDREN'S
MISCELLANY

CHILDREN'S
MISCELLANY

NOTE TO READERS

The publisher and authors disclaim any liability for accidents or injuries that may occur as a result of information given in this book and ask the reader to use common sense to distinguish humor from real advice.

Every effort has been made to ensure that the information in this book is correct at the time of going to press. Nevertheless, some of the information is, by its very nature, anecdotal, changeable or disputable, and cannot therefore be assumed to be authoritative or exhaustive.

The book is, however, guaranteed to be thoroughly enjoyable.

CHILDREN'S MISCELLANY

Useless information that's essential to know

By Matthew Morgan and Samantha Barnes
Illustrated by Niki Catlow

chronicle books · san francisco

First published in the United States in 2005 by
Chronicle Books LLC.

Copyright © 2004 by Buster Books, U.K.
Originally published in Great Britain in 2004 by Buster Books,
an imprint of Michael O'Mara Books Limited, 9 Lion Yard,
Tremadoc Road, London, SW4 7NQ.

Typeset in Langer.
Manufactured in China.

Library of Congress Cataloging-in-Publication Data
Morgan, Matthew.
Children's miscellany : useless information that's essential to know / by
Matthew Morgan and Samantha Barnes ; illustrated by Niki Catlow.
p. cm.
"Read it and be one step ahead of your friends,
parents, teachers, and alligators!"
"Originally published in Great Britain in 2004 by Buster Books"—T.p.
verso.
ISBN 978-0-8118-5067-4
1. Curiosities and wonders—Juvenile literature.
I. Barnes, Samantha. II. Catlow, Niki. III. Title.
AG243.M666 2005
031.02—dc22
2005001090

10 9 8 7 6 5 4

Chronicle Books LLC
680 Second Street, San Francisco, California 94107

www.chroniclekids.com

CONTENTS

CONTENTS

CONTENTS

CONTENTS

CONTENTS

ANIMAL RECORDS

Largest animal	Blue whale 110 ft. (33.5 m), 209 tons
Largest land animal	African bush elephant 13 ft. (3.9 m), 8 tons
Tallest animal	Giraffe 19 ft. (5.8 m)
Largest reptile	Saltwater crocodile 16 ft. (4.9 m), 1,150 lb. (522 kg)
Longest snake	Reticulated python 26–32 ft. (8–10 m)
Longest fish	Whale shark 41.8 ft. (12.7 m)
Largest bird	Ostrich 9 ft. (2.7m), 345 lb. (156.5 kg)
Largest insect	Stick insect 15 in. (38 cm)
Fastest animal	Peregrine falcon 100–200 mph (160–320 kph)
Fastest land animal	Cheetah 70 mph (112 kph)
Fastest insect	Dragonfly 36 mph (57 kph)

SILLY HAIRCUTS

Mullet • Mohican • Skinhead • Hedgehog • Curtains • Bowl • Perm

---IMPORTANT QUESTIONS---

"What is the speed of dark?"

"Why doesn't glue stick to the inside of the bottle?"

'Who put an *s* in the word *lisp*?"

"Why aren't all rooms room temperature?"

"If vegetable oil comes from vegetables,
where does baby oil come from?"

"Why do your feet smell and your nose run?"

"What was the best thing before sliced bread?"

"If an orange is an orange, why isn't a lemon a yellow?"

---HOW TO MILK A COW---

1. Clean your hands.

2. Put a dollop of udder cream on your hands.

3. Take the base of the cow's teat firmly between the last three fingers of your left hand.

4. Draw slightly on the teat and the udder at the same time.

5. Do not jerk or pull – this will irritate the cow and can cause injury.

6. With your right hand, take the base of another teat firmly between the last three fingers and repeat as above.

7. Proceed quickly but gently with each hand until the supply of milk finishes.

Top tip: Never milk a cow when it is eating.

─────── 50 EASILY MISSPELLED WORDS ───────

acceptable	equipment	intelligence	receive
accidentally	exceed	judgment	restaurant
a lot	existence	knowledge	rhythm
argument	experience	leisure	ridiculous
believe	foreign	library	sensible
calendar	fourth	lightning	separate
category	generally	millennium	special
changeable	grammar	mischievous	tomorrow
conscience	grateful	noticeable	twelfth
conscious	guarantee	occasion	weather
definitely	height	pastime	weird
disappear	immediate	pigeon	
embarrass	independent	questionnaire	

"Fifty million, fifty million and one . . ."

If you started counting the moment you were born, and continued counting without stopping until you reached the age of 65, you still would not have counted to a billion.

—————————OFF WITH HIS HEAD!—————————

In the Middle Ages, some prisoners suffered a grisly death by being hung, drawn, and quartered. They were strung up by the neck and, then, while still alive, were disemboweled with a blade and had their entrails burned in front of them. They were then hacked into quarters, as it was thought that dismembering a body would prevent the soul of the victim going to heaven.

Prisoners condemned to death in Mongolia were nailed into wooden boxes and then left on the plains to die of exposure and starvation.

In ancient Rome, prisoners found guilty of parricide (killing a relative) were enclosed in a sack that also contained a dog, a cockerel, a viper, and a monkey, and cast into the river or sea.

During the French Revolution, more than 3,000 people were executed by the guillotine. It became a frightful form of entertainment. Crowds of onlookers would hurl abuse at the prisoners, then rush forward as severed heads were lifted into the air, to try and scoop some of the dripping blood onto handkerchiefs to keep as a souvenir.

—————————GRUESOME METHODS OF EXECUTION—————————

Poisoning

Stoning

Drowning

Boiling in oil

Burning at the stake

Gibbeting (left to rot in an iron cage)

In the Middle Ages, animals were tried in court and publicly executed. Birds, wolves, and insects were found guilty of witchcraft and heresy. The last trial took place in 1740, when a French judge found a cow guilty of sorcery and ordered it to be hanged by the neck until dead.

---EARTH FACTS---

Earth weighs 6,588,000,000,000,000,000,000,000 tons.

The center of Earth is probably made of iron, and it may be hotter there than on the surface of the Sun.

Worldwide, more than 50,000 earthquakes occur every year.

Panama is the only place in the world where you can see the Sun rise on the Pacific Ocean and set on the Atlantic Ocean.

---SAY IT WITH FLOWERS---

Bluebell	Reliability	Iris	Power
Coreopsis	Cheerfulness	Juniper	Protection
Cyclamen	Shyness	Lilac	First love
Daffodil	Regard	Locust	Elegance
Dandelion	Wisdom	Lupin	Imagination
Forget-me-not	True love	Nasturtium	Patience
Fuchsia	Good taste	Rose	Love
Geranium	Comfort	Sycamore	Curiosity
Hollyhock	Ambition	Tulip	Fame
Honeysuckle	Generosity	Violet	Faithfulness

MOST-SPOKEN LANGUAGES

Chinese (Mandarin)...1.034 billion speakers
Hindustani...478 million speakers
Spanish..413 million speakers
English...400 million speakers
Russian..280 million speakers
Arabic..230 million speakers

WEIRD MUSEUMS

Museum of Dog Collars, Leeds Castle, Kent, England

Apple and Pear Museum, Château Bricquebec, France

Circus World Museum, Baraboo, Wisconsin

Museum of Bad Art, Dedham, Massachusetts

Museum of the Mousetrap, Bedwas, Wales, UK

Barbie Doll Hall of Fame, Palo Alto, California

Nut Museum, Old Lyme, Connecticut

World's Smallest Museum (containing one room
of antique telephones), Weslaco, Texas

Cockroach Hall of Fame, Plano, Texas

─────────────── **THE PLANETS** ───────────────

All the planets in our solar system orbit the Sun. Mercury is
closest to the Sun, and Pluto is the farthest away. Earth is the
third planet from the Sun and the fifth largest.

MERCURY: Diameter 3,031 mi. (4,878 km)
• Made of rock • Temperature 662°F (350°C)

VENUS: Diameter 7,521 mi. (12,104 km)
• Made of rock • Temperature 896°F (480°C)

EARTH: Diameter 7,927 mi. (12,756 km)
• Made of rock and water • Temperature 71.6°F (22°C)

MARS: Diameter 4,222 mi. (6,794 km)
• Made of rock • Temperature -9.4°F (-23°C)

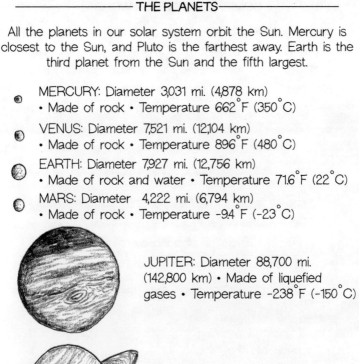

JUPITER: Diameter 88,700 mi.
(142,800 km) • Made of liquefied
gases • Temperature -238°F (-150°C)

SATURN: Diameter 74,900 mi.
(120,536 km) • Made of a solid
core surrounded by liquefied gases
• Temperature -292°F (-180°C)

URANUS: Diameter 31,765 mi. (51,118 km)
• Made of liquefied gases • Temperature -417.2°F (-214°C)

NEPTUNE: Diameter 30,754 mi. (49,492 km)
• Made of liquefied gases • Temperature -428°F (-220°C)

PLUTO: Diameter 1,429 mi. (2,300 km)
• Made of mainly rock • Temperature -446°F (-230°C)

17

——— COMIC-BOOK ACTION WORDS ———

BIFF!	SPLAT!	OOOOF!	SNIKT!
POW!	ZOWIE!	KER-SPLAT!	WAP!
ZZZZAP!	SMASH!	ZANG!	EEYOW!
BOOM!	CRUNCH!	BOP!	THWUNK!
WHAM!	WHIZ!	THOK!	KABOOM!
BANG!	BLAM!	KA-CHOW!	KROOM!

——— DINOSAUR-EXTINCTION THEORIES ———

Meteorite impact • Volcanic gases • Climate cooling
Sea-level change • Changes in the Earth's orbit
Evolution of poisonous fungi

——— I WAS LATE FOR SCHOOL BECAUSE . . . ———

"I squirted the toothpaste too much and spent all morning getting it back into the tube."

"I wanted to make an entrance."

"I'm not late. I thought I'd turn up early for tomorrow."

"My mom forgot to wake me up."

"The bell rang before I got here."

"I was abducted by aliens."

"I invented a time machine that took me forward to my exam results. I get straight As, so I thought I might as well take things easy."

"I'm awake and dressed. What more do you want?"

SECRET LANGUAGES

DOUBLE DUTCH

b — bub	k — kuk	s — sus
c — cash	l — lul	t — tut
d — dud	m — mum	v — vuv
f — fuf	n — nun	w — wash
g — gug	p — pub	x — xux
h — hutch	q — quack	y — yub*
j — jug	r — rug	z — zub

Vowels are pronounced normally.
Example: "Mumarugy hutchadud a lulituttutlule lulamumbub."
(Mary had a little lamb.)

EGGY-PEGGY
Add *egg* before each vowel.
Example: "Meggareggy heggad egga leggittlegge leggamb."

GREE
Add *gree* to the end of every word.
Example: "Marygree hadgree agree littlegree lambgree."

NA
Add *na* to the end of every word.
Example: "Maryna hadna ana littlena lambna."

PIG LATIN
Move the first letter to the end of the word and add *ay* to it.
Example: "Arymay adhay aay ittlelay amblay."

*Y becomes *yub* only when used as a consonant.

The country with the most official languages is the Republic of South Africa. These are English, Afrikaans, isiZulu, isiXhosa, Sesotho, Setswana, Sepedi, Xitsunga, SiSwati, isiNdebele, and Tshivenda.

PRACTICAL JOKES

Find an old rag. Place a coin on the pavement and stand nearby. When a passerby picks the coin up, rip the old rag. The passerby will think they have torn their trousers!

Smudge some dirt on your finger. Tell your friend they have something on their face. Offer to wipe it off for them, and wipe their face with your dirty finger.

Use a pin to prick a hole about an inch from the top of your friend's drinking straw.

Swap the contents of the salt and sugar containers.

Balance a cushion on a partly open door so that when someone walks through it, the cushion lands on their head.

Chew mints, then pretend to bump into a wall. Spit the mints out. People will think you are spitting out your broken teeth!

Record the telephone ringing. Wait for your mom or dad to get into the shower and then play the recording.

CLOSE ENCOUNTERS

Encounters of the First Kind
Reports of objects in the sky or unexplained lights.

Encounters of the Second Kind
Alien spaceship having some kind of tangible effect on Earth's environment, such as burn marks or radioactivity.

Encounters of the Third Kind
Interaction between human witnesses and the crew of an alien spaceship.

Encounters of the Fourth Kind
Immediate human contact with aliens, including transportation.

Encounters of the Fifth Kind
Communication between human beings and aliens.

—————INVENTORS WHO GAVE THEIR NAME—————
TO THEIR INVENTION

Gustave Eiffel	Louis Braille	Earl of Sandwich
EIFFEL TOWER	BRAILLE	SANDWICH
Erno Rubik	George Ferris	Samuel Morse
RUBIK'S CUBE	FERRIS WHEEL	MORSE CODE

When a male tiger and a female lion mate, they produce a tigon. When a female tiger and a male lion mate, they produce a liger. Either way, the offspring are usually sterile.

—————HOW TO FIGHT BACK IN AN—————
ALLIGATOR ATTACK

Use an item of clothing to cover the alligator's eyes.

If you are on land, try to get on the alligator's back and put downward pressure on its neck. This will force its head and jaws down.

Use anything in your possession to hit it, and aim for the eyes and nose.

If the alligator has its jaws around your leg, hit or punch it on the snout.

Seek immediate medical attention to treat any possible infections.

21

INTERNATIONAL DISTRESS SIGNALS

MORSE CODE SIGNALS

— . — . — — . — — . . (CQD)

Said to be "Come Quick Danger"
(officially interpreted as "All Stations: Distress").

. . . — — — . . . (SOS)

Said to be "Save Our Souls" or "Save Our Ship."
The three letters were actually chosen because of
the simple grouping of dots, dashes, and dots, which
were easily recognized in emergencies.

The last distress signal sent by RMS *Titanic* in the
early-morning hours of April 15, 1912, was "SOS." It was
one of the first ships in history to use the new signal.

RADIO SIGNALS

"Mayday! Mayday! Mayday!"

Said three times. From the French *m'aidez,*
meaning "Help me." Used in times of great danger.

"Pan! Pan! Pan!"

Said three times. From the French *panne,*
meaning "breakdown." Used in times of lesser danger.

INSULTS

"You're so fat, if you went to the zoo, the elephants
would start throwing peanuts."

"You're so ugly, when you stand on the beach, the
tide won't come in."

"You're so stupid, you'd try to drown a fish!"

"You're so old, if I told you to act your age, you'd die."

"You're so dumb, you'd trip over a cordless phone!"

MYSTERIES AT SEA

THE *FLYING DUTCHMAN*

The *Flying Dutchman* is a phantom ship condemned to sail the oceans with a ghostly crew. The ship has been sighted many times. The last recorded sighting was in 1942, off the coast of South Africa.

THE BERMUDA TRIANGLE

The Bermuda Triangle is a mysterious area in the Atlantic Ocean where paranormal events and unexplained disappearances are alleged to occur. Some say the Bermuda Triangle is inhabited by monsters that kidnap ships and aircraft.

ATLANTIS

According to ancient myth, Atlantis is the name of a lost island that sank into the ocean after tidal waves covered it in water. Explorers have traveled over the globe in search of traces of its existence, but no real evidence has ever been discovered.

THE *MARY CELESTE*

The *Mary Celeste* was found adrift on the Atlantic Ocean in 1872. The ship was in first-class condition and there was plenty of food and water. The crew, however, had disappeared.

——————— MOST-COMMON SURNAMES———————

China	Li	Russia	Ivanov
France	Martin	Spain	Garcia
Italy	Rossi	Sweden	Johansson
Germany	Müller	U.S./England	Smith
The Netherlands	De Vries	Ireland	Murphy

———————RULING TITLES———————

Emir	Native ruler in parts of Asia and Africa
Emperor/empress	Head of an empire
King	Male sovereign
Pharaoh	Ruler of ancient Egypt
Queen	Female sovereign
Rani	Indian ruler
Shah	Sovereign of Iran
Sultan/sultana	Muslim sovereign
Czar/czarina	Ruler of Russia until 1917

—MONEY EARNERS—

Delivering newspapers
Washing cars
Gardening
Making and selling lemonade
Collecting golf balls
Walking dogs
Running errands
Dishwashing
Cutting grass
Selling cookies
Babysitting

——SANDWICHES——

Cheese and jam
Ketchup and chips
Peanut butter and banana
Pickle and ice cream
Toasted Mars bar
Corn nuts and butter
French fries and
chocolate spread
Tuna, sugar, and vinegar
Egg and pickled onion
Mushy peas and mayonnaise

FIND FIVE FRUITS

Go range through every clime, where'er
The patriot muse appears,
His deeds of valor antedates,
His ban an army fears.

HOW TO ARRANGE AN ORCHESTRA

A – Conductor
B – First violins
C – Second violins
D – Flutes
E – Clarinets
F – Bassoons
G – Oboes
H – Cellos

I – Violas
J – Basses
K – Harp
L – Percussion
M – Horns
N – Trombones
O – Trumpets
P – Tuba

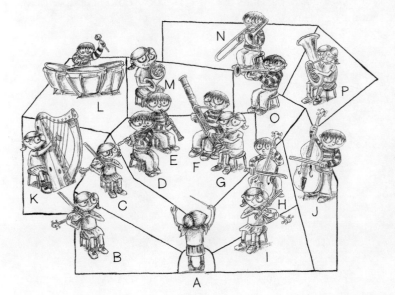

---HUMAN, OR MONKEY?---

Apes and humans share 98 percent of their genetic
material. However, there are some differences:

HUMAN	APE
• Large, variable-sized brain	• Small brain
• Legs longer than arms	• Arms longer than legs
• Feet for walking, not climbing	• Handlike feet with opposable big toes
• Walks upright	• Walks on all fours
• Spine joins skull from below	• Spine joins skull from back
• Knee joints lock upright	• Knee joints will not lock upright
• Short hair over most of the body	• Very hairy body
• Mostly white eyes	• Completely brown eyes
• Vocal cords capable of complex sounds and singing	• Vocal cords capable only of simple sounds

——————HOW TO MAKE A RAINBOW——————

You will need: a sunny day, a glass, white paper, water.

1. Fill a glass with water almost to the top.
2. Place the glass so that it is half on and half off the edge of a table.
3. Place a piece of white paper on the floor.
4. Make sure the sun shines directly through the water onto the white paper.
5. Adjust the paper or the glass until a rainbow forms on the paper.

—————TEN WAYS TO SAVE THE PLANET—————

Volunteer for an environmental charity.

Switch off electrical items when not in use.

Walk or cycle to school instead of being driven.

Take bottles, glass, cans, paper, and plastic to be recycled.

Turn down the heater by one degree.

Use energy-efficient, compact, fluorescent lightbulbs.

Take quick showers rather than deep baths.

Bring reusable bags when shopping.

Use products that are environmentally friendly, such as recycled paper.

Take an interest in environmental issues on television, in magazines, and on the Internet.

———————HORRIBLE SOUNDS———————

Knuckles cracking • Fingernails scratching down a blackboard
Skin rubbing against a balloon • Wool grating between teeth

PIRATE PUNISHMENTS

MAN OVERBOARD

If a pirate was found guilty of a serious crime, he would be forced to walk the plank or flung over the side of the ship. Particularly nasty captains would tow the treacherous pirate behind the ship on a length of rope until he died of hypothermia, exhaustion, or drowning.

MAROONING

Pirates found guilty of mutiny were either left on a remote, deserted island or cast adrift on a tiny raft, with no provisions.

DUNKING

As a less severe punishment, pirates were strung upside down from a mast and lowered down into the ocean several times, then left hung up to dry in the blazing sun.

BIRDS THAT CANNOT FLY

Emu • Kiwi • Ostrich • Dodo • Penguin

—DISGUSTING DISHES FROM AROUND THE WORLD—

JELLIED BLOOD (China)
Congealed duck or pig blood is served on a plate in the shape of a pizza, with herbs and rice crackers.

STINKHEADS (Alaska)
Eskimos chop the heads off raw fish, particularly salmon, bury them in ice for three to four months, then dig them up and eat the foul-smelling result.

DRIED ALGAE (Africa)
The Kanembu, a tribe living on the shores of Lake Chad, harvest a common variety of algae called spirulina, dry it on the sand, mix it up into a spicy cake, and eat it with tomatoes and chili peppers.

MAGGOT CHEESE (Sardinia)
Cheese is left out covered with cheesecloth so flies lay their eggs in it. When the maggots hatch, the resulting mess is spread on bread and devoured.

1,000-YEAR-OLD EGGS
(China)
A duck egg is buried in garden soil for 100 days, then dug up, the shell cracked and removed, and the grayish-green hard yolk cut into slices and served.

BLOOD STEW (Philippines)
This stew is made from pig's heart, liver, head, and blood and is often more pleasantly known as chocolate pork.

---FREAKY FASHIONS---

In Tudor England, people wore huge collars and ruffs around their necks that sometimes stuck out farther than their shoulders.

In Renaissance Italy, women shaved off their eyebrows and shaved their hair several inches back from their natural hairlines.

Fashionable women in medieval Japan gilded or blackened their teeth.

In ancient Rome, women used a paste of chalk mixed with vinegar as perfume.

Some of the earliest cosmetics, made from mercury and lead, disfigured faces and sometimes poisoned people to death.

The hobble skirt, popular in the 19th century, was so narrow below the knees that it made it difficult for women to walk.

The practice of foot binding began in China around 960 B.C. Infant girls had all their toes (except their big toes) broken and their feet bound with cloth strips to stop them from growing larger than about 4 inches. Foot binding ceased in the 20th century.

18th-century hoop petticoats made getting through a door difficult and getting into a carriage almost impossible. If the wearer sat down too fast, the hoop could also fly up and hit her in the face.

In ancient Egypt, rich women placed a large cone of scented grease on top of their heads and kept it there all day. The grease melted and dripped down over their bodies, covering their skin with an oily, fragrant sheen.

—————————KNOCK, KNOCK. WHO'S THERE?—————————

Major..............Major, look, major, stare, major, lose your underwear.

Boo..Don't cry. It's only a joke.

Nunya..Nunya business!

Al.....................Al bust this door down if you don't let me in.

Amanda..A man dat wants to come in.

Toby................................Toby or not Toby, that is the question.

Atch...Bless you!

Albert..Albert you don't know who I am.

Elma...................Elma-ny more knock-knock jokes can you take?

—————————ROMAN NUMERALS—————————

1	I	20	XX	200	CC
2	II	30	XXX	300	CCC
3	III	40	XL	400	CCCC
4	IV	50	L	500	D
5	V	60	LX	600	DC
6	VI	70	LXX	700	DCC
7	VII	80	LXXX	800	DCCC
8	VIII	90	XC	900	CM
9	IX	100	C	1,000	M
10	X				

According to legend, Rome was built by twin brothers, Romulus and Remus. When they were babies, their wicked uncle put them in a basket and left them by the River Tiber to starve. They were rescued and looked after by a she-wolf. Years later, Mars, the god of war, approached the boys and told them to build a city where they had been found. They built the city but ended up at war with each other. Romulus won the battle, and, as a result, the city became known as Rome.

---MARTIAL ARTS---

TAE KWON DO ("The Foot Hand Way")
Origin: Korea • Self-defense
• Emphasizes impressive high kicks
and hand techniques.

KARATE ("Empty Hand")
Origin: Japan • Self-defense • Very
energetic, focuses on strikes and kicks.

KUNG FU ("Skill/Art")
Origin: China • Developed by the
Shaolin monks • Focuses on strikes and
kicks • Develops balance and speed.

JUJITSU ("Soft/Gentle Art")
Origin: Japanese samurai and Chinese
monks • Strikes and throwing
• Uses grappling techniques to turn an
opponent's own strength against them.

AIKIDO ("The Way of the Harmonious Spirit")
Origin: Japan • A mental art of nonresistance • Relies on using
the opponent's own momentum and force against them
through holds, throws, and locks.

JUDO ("The Gentle/Soft Way")
Origin: Japan • A modernized form of jujitsu • Uses leverage
and balance to throw an opponent of any size to the floor.

---HOW MANY DAYS?---

Thirty days hath September,
April, June, and November;
All the rest have thirty-one,
Excepting February alone,
Which has but twenty-eight days clear,
And twenty-nine in each leap year.

GREEK AND ROMAN GODS

GREEK		ROMAN
Aphrodite	Goddess of sensual love and beauty	Venus
Apollo	God of prophecy, healing, and music	Phoebus
Ares	God of war	Mars
Artemis	Goddess of hunting	Diana
Athena	Goddess of war and crafts	Minerva
Demeter	Goddess of agriculture	Ceres
Dionysus	God of wine and ecstasy	Bacchus
Hades	God of the underworld	Pluto
Hephaestus	God of fire	Vulcan
Hera	Queen of heaven	Juno
Hermes	Messenger of the gods	Mercury
Poseidon	God of the sea	Neptune
Zeus	All-powerful father of gods and mortals	Jupiter

Moths are not attracted to light. They fly toward the blackest point; which appears to be behind the light.

HOW TO FIGHT BACK IN A SHARK ATTACK

If a shark attacks you, use anything in your possession to hit the shark. Aim for the shark's eyes or gills, which are the areas most sensitive to pain (unlike the nose, as is often believed). Make quick, sharp, repeated jabs. Hitting the shark tells it that you are not defenseless, which means that it might leave you alone.

Sharks live in every ocean of the world, and shark attack is a potential danger for anyone who swims in shark-inhabited seas. But don't panic—you are much more likely to be struck by lightning than attacked by a shark.

PLAYING CARDS

CLUBS	represent soldiers
DIAMONDS	represent merchants
SPADES	represent the peasant class (who dig for a living)
HEARTS	represent the upper classes (love was considered a concept that could be appreciated only by the rich and educated)

BIG NUMBERS

million	1,000,000
billion	1,000,000,000
trillion	1,000,000,000,000
quadrillion	1,000,000,000,000,000
vigintillion	1 followed by 63 zeros
googol	1 followed by 100 zeros
nonagintillion	1 followed by 273 zeros
centillion	1 followed by 303 zeros

WHAT'S IN AN ITCH?

Sole of foot	You will go traveling.
Right palm	You will make money.
Left palm	You will lose money.
Right eye	You will weep.
Left eye	You will laugh.
Nose	You will have unexpected company.
Lips	You will receive a kiss.
Inside of elbow	Someone will visit you.
Outside of elbow	Someone will leave you.
Right ear	Someone is praising you.
Left ear	Someone is talking ill of you.

──────── LESSONS TO LEARN FROM CARTOONS ────────

When running off a cliff, you will run some way in midair before stopping, looking down, and plummeting to the ground.

When wishing to arrive unnoticed by burrowing underground, you will leave a trail of dirt aboveground for all to see.

If hit in the face with an object (e.g., an iron), your face will flatten and take on the outline of that object.

If you swallow an object (e.g., a birdcage), your body will take on the shape of that object.

When you hit the ground after a fall from a great height, you will create a huge fog of dust and a crater in the ground that is the exact shape of your body.

If you are surprised, your eyes will jump out of their sockets, your feet will come away from the floor, and a trumpet will sound in the background.

If you see someone beautiful, your pupils will turn into hearts and your heart will pump so hard it can be seen moving in and out of your chest.

Whatever you buy or build in order to catch your opponent (especially if bought from Acme) will not work. It is likely to malfunction and cause extensive damage to you.

If run over by heavy machinery, particularly a steamroller, you will be completely flattened. You will, however, be able to pry your flattened shape from the ground by yourself and pop back into shape soon after.

—————————— HOW TO JUGGLE ——————————

ONE-BALL EXERCISE

Throw the ball in an arc from
hand to hand, to about eye level.

TWO-BALL EXERCISE

Toss the ball in your right
hand to your left hand (as
practiced in the one-ball
exercise). When this ball
reaches the highest point in
its arc, throw the second ball
in an arc from your left hand
to your right. Catch the first
in your left hand, then catch
the second in your right hand.
Stop. Practice until you can
do this smoothly.

THREE-BALL EXERCISE

1. Start with two balls in your right hand (ball A and ball B) and
one ball in your left (ball C). Start by throwing the ball in the
front of your right hand (ball A) in an arc to your left hand.

2. When ball A reaches its highest point, throw the ball in your
left hand (ball C) in an arc to your right hand. Catch ball A in
your left hand. This is like the two-ball exercise.

3. When the ball thrown to your right hand reaches the
highest point of its arc, throw ball B from your right hand in
an arc to your left hand. Catch ball C in your right hand.

4. When ball B reaches its highest point, throw the ball in your
left hand (ball A) in an arc to your right hand. Catch ball B in
your left hand.

Good luck—and don't drop the balls!

---RIDDLES---

"What is as big as an elephant but doesn't weigh anything?"
(An elephant's shadow)

"Before Mount Everest was discovered, what was the highest mountain on Earth?"
(Mount Everest—it just hadn't been discovered)

"If two's company and three's a crowd, then what's four and five?"
(Nine)

"I have an eye but cannot see. What am I?"
(A needle)

"How many times can you subtract 5 from 25?"
(Once—after that, you are subtracting it from 20)

"If you had only one match and you entered a room and found an oil burner, a kerosene lamp, and a wood-burning stove, which would you light first?"
(The match)

"I start with T, I end with T, and I am full of T. What am I?"
(A teapot)

---WHAT'S THAT INSECT?---

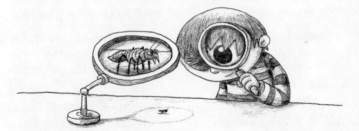

Beetles	Coleoptera
Butterflies and moths	Lepidoptera
Ants, bees, and wasps	Hymenoptera
True flies	Diptera
True Bugs	Hemiptera

THE TEN DEADLIEST SNAKES

FIERCE SNAKE (Australia)
The toxic venom from one
bite would be enough to
kill 100 people.

BROWN SNAKE (Australia)
A drop of venom, smaller
than a grain of salt, could
kill a person.

MALAYAN KRAIT (Asia
and Indonesia)
50 percent of bite
victims have died, even
after treatment.

TIGER SNAKE (Australia)
Extremely aggressive; kills
more people than any
other snake in Australia.

SAW-SCALED VIPER (Africa)
Kills more people than all
other venomous African
snakes combined.

BOOMSLANG (Africa)
Has very long fangs
and can open its mouth
a full 180° to bite.

CORAL SNAKE (US)
Extremely potent venom,
but fangs are typically too
small to pierce human skin.

DEATH ADDER (Australia
and New Guinea)
Can deliver enough venom
in one bite to kill 18 people.

BEAKED SEA SNAKE (Asia)
Responsible for more
than half of all cases
of sea-snake bites, 90
percent of which are fatal.

TAIPAN (Australia)
The venom from one bite
can kill 12,000 guinea pigs.

DANGEROUS JOBS

Formula One driver
Bomb-disposal officer
Test pilot
Special Forces soldier
Circus performer
Stuntperson

Fisher
Miner
Dockworker
Truck driver
Oil-rig worker
Scaffolder

BACK TO FRONT

A palindrome is a word or phrase that is spelled
the same forward as it is backward.

I, madam, I made radio. So I dared. Am I mad, am I?

Neil, an alien?

Marge lets Norah see Sharon's telegram.

Was it a bat I saw?

Madam, I'm Adam.

Oh, who was it I saw? Oh, who?

A man, a plan, a canal, Panama!

Do geese see God?

Mr. Owl ate my metal worm.

A dog! A panic in a pagoda!

Live not on evil.

Did Hannah say as Hannah did?

Stunt nuts!

No melon, no lemon.

Go hang a salami; I'm a lasagna hog.

Ma is as selfless as I am.

Yo! Banana Boy!

Straw warts.

TRAINING YOUR DOG

If possible, start training your dog when it is about 12 weeks old. Be firm and consistent. Always be patient—never shout at or hit your dog.

SHAKING YOUR DOG'S PAW

Your dog should already be able to sit and come to you when called.

1. Get your dog to sit, and offer it a treat.

2. Gently pick up one of its front paws and hold it very loosely in your hand, saying the word "shake" as you do so.

3. Reward your dog immediately with a treat and repeat the exercise several times.

4. Put your hand out and give your dog the chance to put its paw on your open palm when you repeat the command. If it does not do so after a couple seconds, pick up its paw while saying "shake."

5. Repeat. Your dog will get the idea eventually.

BIG SPENDERS

Catherine de' Medici, queen of France, owned a dress worth more than 11 million dollars. She wore it only once.

Queen Elizabeth I of England owned 3,000 gowns.

King Louis XIV of France had 413 beds.

Shah Jahan, emperor of India, spent more than 11 million dollars on his throne. It was 6 ft. (1.82 m) long and 4 ft. (1.22 m) wide, made of solid gold, inlaid with jewels, and covered by a gold canopy fringed with pearls.

Vitellus, emperor of Rome, spent a small fortune on food alone. He often requested 1,000 oysters a day, as well as vast amounts of other delicacies, including pheasant brain and flamingo tongue.

JAPANESE ICE-CREAM FLAVORS

Octopus • Ox tongue • Cactus • Chicken wing • Crab

EDIBLE INSECTS

FRIED GRASSHOPPERS
(China)
Grasshoppers are fried in
sesame oil and eaten like
roasted nuts.

HONEY ANTS
(Australia)
Ants are fed honey until
they swell to twice their
normal size before being
gobbled down raw.

ANT PASTE
(India)
Ants are cooked on a fire,
ground into a paste, salted,
baked, and served as
a chutney.

WITCHETTY GRUBS
(Australia)
Witchetty grubs are beetle
or moth larvae and are best
eaten alive and fresh.

SMART DOGS

The smartest dogs are (in order):

the Border collie
the Poodle
the Golden retriever

The dumbest dog in the world is the Afghan hound.

──────WHAT YOUR DOODLES SAY ABOUT YOU──────

Arrows, ladders, and stairs
You have high aspirations
and a desire to achieve.

Bars and lines
You feel suffocated
and stressed.

Shading
You feel anxious or insecure.

Hearts
You are sentimental
or in love.

Squares and rectangles
You are organized
and efficient.

Sun, moon, and stars
You are optimistic and
likely to succeed.

Animals
You want to protect
someone.

Buildings
You lack stability.

Question marks
You question your role in life.

──────────HOW TO FLY AN AIRPLANE──────────

1. To roll, move the control column left or right. This raises
   a flap on one wing and lowers one on the other.

2. To go up or down, pull or push the control column. This
   raises or lowers a flap on the tailplane.

3. To turn left or right, push the rudder bar or pedals left
   or right with your feet. This turns the upright rudder on the
   tail fin of the aircraft.

4. To bank in a curve (like on a bike when you go around a
   corner), use the control column and the rudder pedals
   together so that the aircraft turns and partly rolls at the
   same time.

---LUDICROUS LAWS---

IN SWEDEN
It is illegal for parents to insult their children.

IN CHINA
It is against the law to save a drowning person, as such an act would interfere with his or her fate.

IN FRANCE
It is illegal for anyone to park or land a flying saucer in a vineyard.

IN GREECE
If you are poorly dressed when driving on the public roads of Athens, your license may be taken away.

IN SWITZERLAND
After 10 p.m., a man or boy cannot relieve himself standing up.

IN SAUDI ARABIA
It is illegal for women to drive cars.

---THE THERMOMETER---

Freezing point of water	$32°F$ ($0°C$)
Boiling point of water	$212°F$ ($100°C$)
Human body	$98.6°F$ ($37°C$)
Hypothermia (body too cold)	$95°F$ (below $35°C$)
Hyperthermia (body too hot)	$104°F$ (above $40°C$)
Butter melts	$88°F$ ($30.6°C$)
Room temperature	$68°F$ ($20°C$)

You can convert a Fahrenheit temperature into a Celsius temperature using math: Subtract $32°$, multiply by 5, and divide by 9.

To convert Celsius into Fahrenheit, multiply by 9, divide by 5, and add $32°$.

STAR SIGNS

SIGN	SYMBOL	ELEMENT	DATES
Aries	Ram	Fire	March 21—April 20
Taurus	Bull	Earth	April 21—May 21
Gemini	Twins	Air	May 22—June 21
Cancer	Crab	Water	June 22—July 22
Leo	Lion	Fire	July 23—Aug. 23
Virgo	Virgin	Earth	Aug. 24—Sept. 23
Libra	Scales	Air	Sept. 24—Oct. 23
Scorpio	Scorpion	Water	Oct. 24—Nov. 22
Sagittarius	Archer	Fire	Nov. 23—Dec. 21
Capricorn	Goat	Earth	Dec. 22—Jan. 20
Aquarius	Water carrier	Air	Jan. 21—Feb. 19
Pisces	Fish	Water	Feb. 20—March 20

ARIES—energetic and enthusiastic, but can be blunt.

TAURUS—confident and artistic, but can be unforgiving.

GEMINI—talkative and charming, but can be careless.

CANCER—sensitive, kind, and loyal, but can be moody.

LEO—sociable and generous, but can be boastful.

VIRGO—dependable and loyal, but can be shy.

LIBRA—balanced and helpful, but can be indecisive.

SCORPIO—determined and fearless, but can be spiteful.

SAGITTARIUS—optimistic and energetic, but can be impulsive.

CAPRICORN—loyal and humorous, but can be oversensitive.

AQUARIUS—inquisitive and precise, but can be stubborn.

PISCES—imaginative and agreeable, but can over-exaggerate.

COMMON PHOBIAS

Spiders..Arachnophobia

People and social situations....................................Sociophobia

Flying...Aerophobia

Open spaces...Agoraphobia

Confined spaces...Claustrophobia

Heights..Acrophobia

Vomiting...Emetophobia

Strangers..Xenophobia

Thunderstorms..Brontophobia

Death...Necrophobia

MAKING FIRE

Twirling a dry twig through a hole in a plank of
wood or in a tree trunk will produce enough heat to
set fire to dry moss.

Cutting a slot into a piece of bamboo and wearing this
slot down with another piece of bamboo will work off
fragments of the wood. The friction will set these
shavings on fire.

Striking a stone against a flint will cause sparks to
fall that can set fire to dry moss.

---------------------ANIMAL FAMILIES---------------------

ANIMAL	MALE	FEMALE	YOUNG
Bear	Boar	Sow	Cub
Horse	Stallion	Mare	Foal
Ferret	Hob	Jill	Kit
Fox	Reynard	Vixen	Cub
Duck	Drake	Duck	Duckling
Hawk	Tercel	Hen	Eyas
Tiger	Tiger	Tigress	Cub
Alligator	Bull	Cow	Hatchling
Dog	Dog	Bitch	Puppy
Red deer	Stag	Hind	Fawn
Goat	Billy	Nanny	Kid
Swan	Cob	Pen	Cygnet

---------------------BLOOD TYPES---------------------

The four best-known human blood types are A, B, AB, and O. Types A and O are the most common. Type AB is the rarest. Blood type, like eye color, is inherited.

Legend has it that blood types reflect personalities:

A	calm and trustworthy
B	creative and excitable
AB	thoughtful and emotional
O	confident and leaderly

The Japanese ask, "What's your blood type?" as others ask, "What's your sign?"

Mosquitos kill more people on Earth than any other animal, because they transmit malaria and other diseases. Worldwide, one person dies of malaria every ten seconds.

MAD MONARCHS

The Pekingese dog was so sacred to Chinese royalty that some even had private palaces, complete with servants.

The ancient Greek leader Pericles was so self-conscious about his pointed head that he would pose for portraits only when wearing a helmet.

The favorite pastime of Emperor Ferdinand of Austria was to wedge himself in a wastepaper basket and roll on the floor. His sister, Marianna, was also mad and usually kept locked up.

Charles VI, or Charles the Mad, ruled France from 1380 to 1422. At times, he feared that he was made of glass, and put iron rods into his clothing to prevent himself from breaking.

Queen Christina of Sweden, who succeeded her father, Gustavus Adolphus, in 1632, was said to be so terrified of fleas that she ordered the construction of a tiny cannon so that she could fire miniature cannonballs at the fleas that infested her bedchamber.

Nabonidus, king of Babylon, is said to have been mentally unstable, and ate grass because he thought he was a goat.

Caligula, emperor of Rome, is said to have made his horse, Incitatus, a member of the Senate, and wanted to have him made consul.

FAMOUS INSOMNIACS

Marilyn Monroe • Charles Dickens • Winston Churchill
Napoleon Bonaparte • Vincent van Gogh

SPACE TERMS

GALAXY
An enormous group of stars, dust, and gas.

PULSAR
A massively dense, spinning neutron star that sends beams of radiation across space.

SUPERNOVA
A star that explodes when it runs out of fuel and burns out.

NEBULA
A glowing cloud heated by newly hatched stars called protostars when they first start to shine.

BLACK HOLE
A hole in space with such a strong gravitational pull that even light cannot escape it.

COMET
A vaporizing ball of ice with a long, luminous tail.

SOLAR SYSTEM
The group of planets, asteroids, and comets held together by the gravitational pull of the Sun.

METEOR
Matter that brightens as it enters Earth's atmosphere; commonly known as a shooting star.

SPACED OUT

The supernova Zeta Thauri was so bright when it exploded in 1054 that it could be seen during the day.

If a pulsar the size of a coin landed on Earth, it would weigh approximately 100 million tons.

Sirius, the Dog Star, is the brightest star we can see and is thought to be 23 times brighter than the Sun.

Five times as many meteors can be seen after midnight as can be seen before.

Saturn's rings are 500,000 miles in circumference but only about 1 ft. (30 cm) thick.

The star Antares is 60,000 times larger than the Sun. If the Sun were the size of a soccer ball, Antares would be as large as a house.

HOW TO ANNOY SOMEONE

Shout out random numbers while they're counting.

Arrange to see them on April 31.

Ask if you can borrow their pen to chew.

Tell them that you exist only in their imagination.

Drum on anything you can find and on every available surface.

Pretend to wipe their spit off your face whenever they speak.

Learn Morse code and communicate only in dots and dashes.

Whistle in their ear. When they ask you to stop, burp
in their ear.

Finish every sentence with the words "as only a true
poet could say."

Never make eye contact. Alternatively, never break eye
contact. Or have one eye do each.

An electric eel can produce a shock of more than 600 volts
— five times as powerful as domestic current in the United
States. It uses this power not only to kill its prey but to locate
it as well. Electric eels are blind, and use electric pulses to
navigate in much the same way as humans uses radar.

WORLD POPULATION

1 billion	1804	4 billion	1974
2 billion	1927	5 billion	1987
3 billion	1960	6 billion	1999

PARTY
THIS WAY →

(true flies
only)

Mayflies and fruit flies are not true flies. True flies have only two wings – all other flying insects have four.

-LARGEST DESERTS-

Sahara (Africa)
Australian
Gobi (Mongolia and China)
Kalahari (Africa)
Turkestan (Asia)
Takla Makan (China)
Sonoran (US)
Namib (Africa)
Thar (India)

-LARGEST DESSERTS-

Residents of Fort Payne, Alabama, made a cake weighing 128,238 lb., 8 oz. (58.08 tons), including 16,209 lb. (7.35 tons) of icing, on October 18, 1989.

Students at Clarendon College, Nottingham, England, made a trifle that weighed 6,896 lb. (3.13 tons), on September 26, 1990.

The richest man in the world is Bill Gates, the founder of computer giant Microsoft. He dropped out of college and became a self-made billionaire. Gates is worth $47 billion.

---ICEBERGS---

Icebergs vary in size, from growlers (about the size of a small car) to masses hundreds of miles wide. The world's largest icebergs are found in the Antarctic Ocean, which also contains 93 percent of the world's mass of icebergs. The largest known iceberg was 207 mi. (333 km) long and 62 mi. (100 km) wide, measured by the icebreaker USS *Glacier* in 1956.

---AMAZING STRENGTH---

American strongman Frank Richards could withstand a cannonball fired at his stomach.

Thomas Topham, who lived in England in the 18th century, could snap his fingers while a man danced on each of his outstretched arms.

Aiyavuk ("Shining Moon"), a Tartar princess of the 13th century, would wrestle with every man who wanted to marry her and claim 100 horses when they failed to beat her. By the time she was 30, she had acquired 10,000 horses.

---THANK YOU---

English	"Thank you"	Italian	"Grazie"
Cantonese	"Doh je"	Japanese	"Arigato"
Greek	"Efharisto"	Portuguese	"Obrigado"
Danish	"Tak"	Norwegian	"Takk"
Russian	"Spasibo"	French	"Merci"
Finnish	"Kiitos"	Polish	"Dziekuje"
German	"Danke"	Spanish	"Gracias"
Indonesian	"Terima kasih"	Czech	"Dêkuji"
Swedish	"Tack"	Hebrew	"Toda"

---------------- HISTORY OF THE CIRCUS ----------------

1768 British soldier and
cavalryman Philip
Astley brings together
the elements of a circus,
with a ring, animals,
strongmen, and jugglers.

1793 John Bill Ricketts stages
America's first circus
in Philadelphia.

1810 Traveling menageries
become popular, containing rare, exotic beasts.

1825 J. Purdy Brown orders the first canvas tent for
his circus.

1829 Trained-animal acts begin to appear at circuses.

1835 Circus wagons appear in circus parades.

1872 Phineas Taylor Barnum moves his entire show in
railroad cars.

1882 Jumbo the elephant is brought to the United States
by the Barnum and London Show.

1883 William F. Cody, or Buffalo Bill, performs in the
first Wild West show, at the Rocky Mountain and
Prairie Exhibition.

1924 The Seils-Sterling circus takes to the road in
motorized vehicles.

1938 The Bertram Mills Circus broadcasts live on TV from
Olympia, London.

1941 Walt Disney Pictures releases *Dumbo*.

1968 Ringling Bros. and Barnum and Bailey open a
clown college.

1974 Philippe Petit walks a tightrope strung between the
World Trade Center's twin towers, 1,350 ft. (411 m) high.

1984 Cirque du Soleil is founded by Guy Laliberte.

———————CIRCUS PERFORMERS———————

Trapeze artist • Tightrope walker • Fire eater • Stilt walker
Clown • Unicyclist • Acrobat • Ringmaster • Animal trainer

———————ALL-TIME BEST-SELLING BOOKS———————

1. The Bible	6 billion-plus
2. *Quotations from Chairman Mao Tse-Tung*	900 million-plus
3. *The Lord of the Rings*	100 million-plus
4. *The American Spelling Book*	up to 100 million
5. *The Guinness Book of Records*	92 million-plus

Females are not allowed on the Greek peninsula of Mount Athos or inside the 20 monasteries located there. Men can enter but not women; roosters but not hens; horses but not mares; bulls but not cows.

———PEOPLE WITH COUNTRIES NAMED AFTER THEM———

Amerigo Vespucci (Italy, 1451–1512)...the United States of America

Ibn Saud (Nejd, 1882–1953)......................................Saudi Arabia

Simón Bolívar (Venezuela, 1783–1830)...........................Bolivia

Christopher Columbus (Italy, 1451–1506)..............Colombia

Philip II (Spain, 1527–1598).................................the Philippines

——THE SEVEN WONDERS OF THE ANCIENT WORLD——

Great Pyramids, Egypt
Hanging Gardens of Babylon, Iraq
Statue of Zeus at Olympia, Greece
Temple of Artemis at Ephesus, Turkey
Mausoleum at Halicarnassus, Turkey
Colossus, Rhodes
Pharos of Alexandria, Egypt

——THE SEVEN—— SEAS	——THE SEVEN—— DEADLY SINS	——THE SEVEN—— DWARFS
Antarctic Ocean	Pride	Bashful
Arctic Ocean	Greed	Doc
North Atlantic Ocean	Lust	Dopey
South Atlantic Ocean	Envy	Grumpy
Indian Ocean	Gluttony	Happy
North Pacific Ocean	Anger	Sleepy
South Pacific Ocean	Sloth	Sneezy

———————ANIMAL GANGS———————

A pack of wolves
A skulk of foxes
A harras of horses
A trip of goats
A murder of crows
A knot of toads
A colony of bats
A band of gorillas
A sloth of bears
An army of caterpillars

A school of fish
A smack of jellyfish
A pride of lions
A labor of moles
A harvest of mice
A gaggle of geese
A mob of kangaroos
A pod of whales
A parliament of owls
A crash of rhinoceroses

──────── FASTEST ROLLER-COASTERS ───────

Top Thrill Dragster, US	120 mph (193 kph), built 2003
Dodonpa, Japan	107 mph (172 kph), built 2001
Superman the Escape, US	100 mph (161 kph), built 1997
Tower of Terror, Australia	100 mph (161 kph), built 1997
Steel Dragon 2000, Japan	95 mph (153 kph), built 2000

──────────── THE MESOZOIC ERA ──────────

Triassic period	208–245 million years ago
Jurassic period	145–208 million years ago
Cretaceous period	65–145 million years ago

When the Triassic period began, there was only one continent on earth, now called Pangaea. This separated into two lesser continents, Laurasia and Gondwanaland, during the Jurassic period, and, during the Cretaceous period, the continents we know today began to appear. This movement is known as continental drift. The continents we know today are moving 1-3 inches (25-75 mm) per year. These changes are fairly insignificant over a human's lifetime, but over the course of hundreds of millions of years, they are very significant.

TIPS FOR MAGICIANS

Practice in front of a mirror so that you can see the magic trick the way your audience will.

Think about what you want to say while performing your trick; talking will distract the audience's attention just enough to keep them puzzling over how you perform your magic!

Never reveal how a trick works.

Never perform the same trick twice to the same audience.

Set up the seating arrangements before a show — many tricks require the audience to be looking directly at you.

When you can, borrow your props (such as coins and pencils) from the audience so they know the items are genuine.

WORLD BODY LANGUAGE

IN HONG KONG
It is rude to beckon someone with your finger. You signal to a person by reaching out, palm down, and fluttering your fingers.

IN PAKISTAN
It is rude to show the soles of your feet or point a foot when sitting on the floor.

IN SRI LANKA
Shaking your head means yes, and nodding it up and down means no.

IN JAPAN
Women cover their mouths when they laugh because it is rude to show their teeth.

IN CHILE
Slapping your right fist into your left palm is obscene, and an open palm with the fingers separated means "stupid."

IN BELGIUM
It is considered rude to put your hands in your pockets while talking to someone.

If your shoes smell, sprinkle a little baking soda into them and leave it overnight before removing.

────────── MAGIC-HANDCUFF TRICK ──────────

You will need: a piece of rope about 3 ft. (1 m) long, a large scarf, two identical bracelets, a long-sleeved top.

Setup: Slide one bracelet up your arm, making certain it is hidden beneath your sleeve.

PERFORMANCE

1. Ask two helpers to tie the ends of the rope to your wrists.

2. Ask one helper to pass you the bracelet, then tell the audience that you will make this appear on the rope with your hands still tied.

3. Tell your helpers to cover your hands with the scarf. They should continue to hold up the ends of the scarf.

4. With your hands out of sight, hide the bracelet in your pocket or under your clothes. Then slide the hidden bracelet down your sleeve on top of the rope.

5. Now ask your helpers to take the scarf away. Hold up your arms and show the bracelet dangling from the rope.

Egyptians often brought a giant mummy to banquets to remind everyone that death was never far away.

MAGICAL CREATURES

Brownie......................................Good-natured and helpful house fairy

Changeling....................Fairy child left in the place of a human baby

Gnome...................Bearded man who guards treasure underground

Goblin...........................Mischievous and naughty household creature

Leprechaun................................Small, roguish man dressed in green

Pixie...Small spirit that loves to play tricks

Troll.............................Flesh-eating creature that lives in dark places

Vila.............Nymph of woods and streams who foretells the future

Dwarf........................Small, bearded miner who makes magical gifts

Ogre.................................Giant, hideous monster of extreme stupidity

REAL CHIP FLAVORS

Popcorn • Seaweed • Hamburger • Hedgehog
Pizza • Greek kebab • Octopus • Creamy stew
Spicy pork rind • Sour cream and squid • Banana

Research indicates that mosquitoes are attracted
to people who have recently eaten bananas.

NOT ALLOWED

Unmarried women parachuting on Sundays (Florida).

Persons classified as ugly walking down any street (San Francisco).

Taking a bite from another person's hamburger (Oklahoma).

Singing in a public place when wearing a swimsuit (Florida).

Carrying an ice-cream cone in your back pocket (Alabama).

Getting a fish drunk (Ohio).

Milking another person's cow (Texas).

Donkeys sleeping in bathtubs (Arizona).

Taking more than three sips of beer while standing (Texas).

Wearing a false mustache that may cause people to laugh in church (Alabama).

DINOSAURS

Longest	Seismosaurus	150 ft. (45 m)
Heaviest	Argentinasaurus	220,000 lb. (100 kg)
Smallest	Micropachycephalosaurus	24 in. (61 cm)
Longest horn	Triceratops	40 in. (1 m)
Longest claw	Therizonasaurus	27 in. (70 cm)
Longest neck	Sauroposeidon	49.2 ft. (15 m)
Biggest head	Pentaceratops	9.8 ft. (3 m)
Longest teeth	Tyrannosaurus rex	7 in. (18 cm)
Most vicious	Utah raptor	

BALLET TERMS

GLISSADE
Gliding

PIROUETTE
Complete turn on one leg

ARABESQUE
Standing on one leg and
leaning forward with the
other leg stretched back

ENTRECHAT
Crossing and uncrossing
of feet during a jump

JETÉ
Jumping from one foot
to the other

POINTE
Dancing on tiptoes

PLIÉ
Bending knees

LIGHTNING

Lightning is a long spark of electrical energy that travels
through the air to relieve the excess of electrical charge
within a cloud. It is estimated that, on Earth, 100 lightning
flashes occur every second.

The temperature of a flash of lightning can reach $50,000°F$
$(28,000°C)$, Earth's highest naturally occurring temperature,
which is five times hotter than the surface of the Sun.

Cloud-to-Earth flashes actually consist of two flashes, the
first from the cloud to the ground and a return flash
from the ground to the cloud.

The safest place to be when lightning strikes is indoors or
in a low, sunken area such as a ditch.

Thunder is caused by the rapid heating of the air by lightning.
The air around the lightning flash expands at supersonic
speeds, creating a series of claps and rumbles.

────HOW TO MAKE YOUR OWN LIGHTNING────

You will need: a balloon, wool clothing (such as a sweater), a metal surface (such as a filing cabinet).

1. Inflate the balloon.

2. Darken the room as much as possible.

3. Rub the balloon against the wool sweater about ten times.

4. Move the balloon close to the metal surface.

The balloon is being used to create static electricity. A flash or spark will jump, like lightning, from the balloon to the metal surface.

──────────NAMES FOR SANTA CLAUS────── AROUND THE WORLD

United States	Santa Claus
United Kingdom	Father Christmas
Brazil	Papai Noel
Hungary	Mikulas (St. Nicholas)
China	Che Dun Lao Ren (Christmas Old Man)
Russia	Ded Moroz (Grandfather Frost)
France	Père Noël
Germany	Weihnachtsmann (Christmas Man)
Italy	Babbo Natale
Hawaii	Kanakaloka
Japan	Hoteiosho (a god who bears gifts)
Chile	Viejo Pascuero (Old Man Christmas)
Poland	Swiety Mikolaj (St. Nicholas)
The Netherlands	Sinterklaas
Sweden	Jultomten (Christmas Brownie)
Norway	Julenissen (Christmas Gnome)
Finland	Joulupukki (Old Man Christmas)

─────STARE AT THE BLACK DOT─────

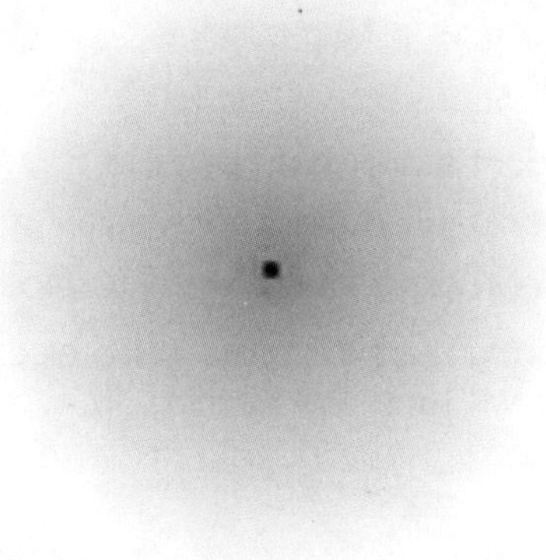

After a while the gray haze
around it will start to shrink.

─────CLOUD TYPES─────

HIGH CLOUDS

Cirrus	Wisps of ice crystals
Cirrocumulus	Ripples of small, fleecy cloud
Cirrostratus	Cloud veil, halo phenomenon

MIDDLE CLOUDS

Altocumulus	Layers or rolls of fluffy cloud
Altostratus	Gray or white sheets
Nimbostratus	Gray rain clouds

LOW CLOUDS

Stratocumulus	Layer at top of cumulus
Stratus	Gray cloud layer
Cumulus	Large, white fluffy cloud
Cumulonimbus	Dark storm cloud with rain

BEAUFORT SCALE

Francis Beaufort was born in 1774 in County Meath, Ireland. He became a cabin boy at 13 and realized that it was important to be aware of weather conditions while at sea. He kept a journal of the weather his whole life and invented the Beaufort scale in 1806. The British Royal Navy adopted his method in 1838, and it is now the international measure of weather at sea.

0	Calm	7	Near gale
1	Light air	8	Gale
2	Light breeze	9	Strong gale
3	Gentle breeze	10	Storm
4	Moderate breeze	11	Violent storm
5	Fresh breeze	12	Hurricane
6	Strong breeze		

HURRICANES

Hurricanes are classified into five categories, based on their wind speeds and potential to cause damage.

Category one	Winds 74–95 mph (119–153 kph)
Category two	Winds 96–110 mph (154–177 kph)
Category three	Winds 111–130 mph (178–209 kph)
Category four	Winds 131–155 mph (210–249 kph)
Category five	Winds over 155 mph (250 kph)

The parachute was invented more than 100 years before the airplane. It was a creation of Frenchman Louis-Sebastien Lenormand, who designed it in 1783 to save people who jumped from burning buildings. He demonstrated the principle by jumping from a tree with two parasols.

---HOW TO DO A WHEELIE---

A wheelie is difficult to perform on a road bike. It is easier on a BMX-style bike because of the lower center of gravity.

1. Sit on the bike.

2. Start pedaling until you get to about 5 mph (8 kph).

3. Stand on the pedals.

4. Lean back over the rear wheel.

5. Pull sharply on the handlebar while still pedalling.

6. As the front wheel rises, balance your weight and your pedaling to maintain the wheelie.

   Top tip: Keep your wheel at a good height and be careful not to flip over onto your back – touching the back brake will help prevent this.

---BIRTHSTONES---

January	Garnet
February	Amethyst
March	Bloodstone
April	Diamond
May	Emerald
June	Pearl
July	Ruby
August	Sardonyx
September	Sapphire
October	Opal
November	Topaz
December	Turquoise

──────SECRET ALPHABET CODE──────

26	A	19	H	12	O	5	V
25	B	18	I	11	P	4	W
24	C	17	J	10	Q	3	X
23	D	16	K	9	R	2	Y
22	E	15	L	8	S	1	Z
21	F	14	M	7	T		
20	G	13	N	6	U	↲	

To spell a word, write out each letter as the number that corresponds to it on the chart above. If you need to use numbers in your message, spell them out or it will spoil the code.

──────────── WEATHER PREDICTIONS ────────────

You can predict certain weather with about 80 percent accuracy by monitoring the croaks of frogs. If frogs croak on a fine day, it will rain in two days. If frogs croak after rain, there will be fine weather. It will continue to rain if frogs do not croak after successive wet days.

The outdoor temperature can be estimated to within several degrees by timing the chirps of a cricket. Count the number of chirps in a 15-second period and add 37 to the total. The result will be very close to the Fahrenheit temperature.

Poplar trees and red and silver maples flip their leaves up when air pressure is low and rain is on its way.

Many people can smell rain coming. Some scientists believe moisture and impending rain make your nose more sensitive.

You can determine how far away lightning is by counting the number of seconds between the flash of lightning and the sound of thunder. Divide the amount by two to reveal how many miles away the lightning is. If you see lightning and hear thunder simultaneously, you're right in the middle of the storm.

ARE THESE LINES HORIZONTAL?

During your lifetime, you will eat about 60,000 pounds
of food—the weight of about six elephants!

ANCIENT EGYPTIAN GODS

Some images of ancient Egyptian gods and goddesses show
them with a human body and the head of a bird or an animal.
Animals were chosen to represent the powers of the god.

Amon	King of the gods	Head of a ram
Anubis	God of mummification	Head of a jackal
Bast	Goddess of protection	Head of a cat
Geb	Earth god	Head of a goose
Hathor	Sky goddess	Head of a cow
Sekhmet	Goddess of war and battle	Head of a lioness
Horus	God of the Egyptians	Head of a falcon
Heket	Goddess of childbirth	Head of a frog
Tefnut	Goddess of the rain	Head of a lioness
Thoth	God of wisdom	Head of an ibis bird
Sebek	God of swift action	Head of a crocodile

—WILD LIFE SPANS—

Giant tortoise............200 years
Box turtle....................100 years
Gray parrot.................90 years
Human...........................80 years
Swan.............................70 years
Alligator........................60 years
Elephant......................50 years
Chimpanzee................40 years
Lion..............................30 years
Sheep..........................20 years
Rabbit..........................10 years
Chipmunk.....................5 years
Guinea pig....................4 years
Mouse...........................3 years
House spider.................4 days
Mayfly...........................1 day

The average hummingbird weighs less than a small coin. Its newborn are the size of tiny moths and its nest is the size of a walnut.

TEETH

Teeth consist of three layers:

• An outer layer of enamel covers part or all of the crown of the tooth.

• The middle layer is called dentine, which is less hard than the enamel.

• The dentine is nourished by an inner layer, the pulp, which consists of cells, tiny blood vessels, and the nerve.

Humans have two sets of teeth during life. The first set of teeth are called primary, or milk, teeth, and the second set are called permanent, or adult, teeth. Humans have 20 primary and 32 permanent teeth.

——— GOOD LUCK ———

Stroking a black cat.

Finding a four-leaf clover.

Hanging a horseshoe above
a door.

Carrying a hare's foot.

Finding a coin heads up.

Wearing new clothes
at Easter.

Seeing a chimney sweep.

Finding a frog or cricket
in the house.

——— BAD LUCK ———

Seeing three butterflies
together.

Letting milk boil over.

Stepping on a crack
in the pavement.

Walking under a ladder.

Breaking a mirror.

Opening an umbrella indoors.

Leaving a house through a
different door than the one
through which you entered.

—PREHISTORIC LIFE— THAT EXISTS TODAY

Australian lungfish

Cunglio tree

Horseshoe crab

Turtle

Crocodile

Duck-billed platypus

Peripatus worm

——MINERAL—— MADNESS

There is enough phosphorus in the human body to make the heads of 2,000 matches.

There is enough iron in the human body to make a nail.

There is enough carbon in the human body to make the lead for 9,000 pencils.

—————DEAD STRANGE—————

The Greek playwright Aeschylus died after being hit on the head by a tortoise that had been dropped by a passing eagle.

Arnold Bennett, an English novelist, drank a glass of water to prove it was safe. The glass of water gave him typhoid, which killed him.

Attila the Hun, famous for his ferocity in battle, died from a nosebleed.

The Danish astronomer Tycho Brahe died after his bladder burst at dinner. He thought it would have been rude to have excused himself to use the toilet before the meal was over.

The French composer Jean-Baptiste Lully got so engrossed in rehearsal with his musicians that he drove his baton through his foot and later died of an infection.

—————FAMOUS VEHICLES—————

Herbie • Chitty Chitty Bang Bang • Batmobile • KITT
Mystery Machine • Thomas the Tank Engine • Tardis
Enterprise • Broom • Fab One • Budgie
Millennium Falcon • Hogwarts Express

GREAT ACHIEVEMENTS OF THE ANCIENT EGYPTIANS

The Great Pyramids

The creation of written history

The invention of paper made from papyrus

The invention of hieroglyphic writing

The creation of the first calendar known to use
a year of 365 days, approximately equal to the
solar year or year of the seasons

HOW TO DO A BUNNY HOP

Wear kneepads, elbowpads, gloves, and a fitted helmet for
safety. A BMX-style bike is easiest to use.

1. Stand on the bike's pedals.

2. Start pedaling until you get to about 5 mph (8 kph).

3. Level the pedals so that your feet are even and parallel
   to the ground.

4. Press down on the handlebars and pedals.

5. Lessen the pressure of your feet and hands slightly, but
   maintain contact between yourself and the bike.

6. "Hop" into the air.

HOW TO SPOT A . . .

WITCH	WEREWOLF	VAMPIRE
pointy shoes	excessive hair	fangs
warts	fear of full moons	no reflection
cackly laugh	long fingernails	long coat
dislike of children	howls	pale complexion
broomstick	yellow eyes	may try to bite

---WAR---

SHORTEST

The shortest war was between England and Zanzibar. It took place on August 27, 1896, and lasted 38 minutes, from 9:02 a.m. to 9:40 a.m.

LONGEST

The Hundred Years War lasted 116 years, between 1337 and 1453.

DEADLIEST

It is estimated that World War II took up to 56.4 million lives.

---NIGHTTIME DISTURBANCES---

Sleep talking
(Somniloquy)

Bed wetting
(Enuresis)

Lack of breath
(Sleep apnea)

Sleepwalking
(Somnambulism)

Teeth grinding
(Bruxism)

Sleeplessness
(Insomnia)

---ANIMAL HOMES---

Badger	Sett	Hare	Form
Bat	Roost	Otter	Holt
Bear	Den	Rabbit	Warren
Beaver	Lodge	Squirrel	Drey
Fox	Earth	Mole	Hole

George Washington wore dentures made of wood. They tasted so horrible that he soaked them in port at night.

--------------------- THE CONTINENTS ---------------------

Africa • Asia • Australia

Europe • Antarctica • America

The first letter of each continent's
name is the same as its last.

Asia has the largest land area, the largest population,
and the highest mountains.

Australia is the smallest continent.

Europe has the highest ratio of coastline to total area.

----------------------- EXPLORERS -----------------------

982   Greenland is discovered by the Viking Eric the Red.

1002   Eric the Red's son, Leif the Lucky, discovers
         North America.

1271–95 Marco Polo journeys to China, establishing the
         overland trade route. He leaves China in 1292
         and arrives home three years later.

1432   Portuguese navigators discover the Azores.

1470–84 Portuguese explorers discover Africa's Gold Coast
         and the Congo River.

1492   Christopher Columbus firsts sets sail to reach Asia.
         In four voyages, he discovers the Bahamas,
         Hispaniola, Dominica, Jamaica, Guadeloupe, Cuba,
         Central America, and South America.

1497–8   Vasco da Gama rounds the Cape of Good Hope
         and reaches India.

1519   Ferdinand Magellan, who gave the Pacific Ocean its
         name, leads the first expedition to sail around the
         world. The voyage takes three years and is
         completed by Juan Sebastian del Cano.

1770   James Cook lands in Australia.

—————————HOW TO ANNOY SOMEONE (2) ———————

Speak only in a robot voice.

Only say, "I wouldn't expect you to understand."

Shout the word "Boring!" every time they start to speak.

Point at their knees, mumbling, "Cheese knees" and "Mmm, interesting."

Point a remote control at them and press "Stop" whenever they start talking.

Repeat everything they say, adding the word "echo" at the end.

Don't reply. Instead, keep handing them pieces of string, telling them, "I am Spider-Man."

Ask, "Do you hear that?" They say, "What?" You say, "Never mind, it's gone now." Repeat. A lot.

When they are talking to you, stare at a certain spot on their face and look puzzled or shocked.

——————————MOST DISGUSTING SMELLS ——————————

Feet
Poo
Eggs
Sick
Cheese
Rotten fish
Drains
Skunks
Pigs
Wet dogs
Dog breath

THINGS NOT TO HAVE A BATH IN

Baked beans	Eels	Manure
Ice cubes	Seaweed	Vegetable soup
Paint	Slugs	Custard

THINGS NOT TO DO AFTER BATHING

Roll in mud   Change a lightbulb   Forget your towel

AGE OF EXPLORATION

Early adventurers were motivated by many things, including a desire for conquest and a hunger for gold. Sometimes the country they were seeking existed only in legend or rumor. The crewmen on these long and dangerous voyages were not always experienced seamen, and great numbers were employed, as many would be lost to illness and death.

Cooking was seldom done at sea. Food stores often consisted of pickled or dried meat and ship's biscuits, made from flour and water. By the end of the voyage, these biscuits would be full of black insects called weevils.

PALMISTRY

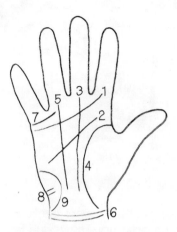

1. HEART LINE
Straight: Romantic
Long: Outgoing
Short: Shy

2. HEAD LINE
Curved: Spontaneous
Straight: Practical
Deep: Imaginative

3. FATE LINE
To have a fate line shows a sense of responsibility and purpose.

4. LIFE LINE
Long: Vitality for life
Short: Good health
Weak: Indecisive

5. SUN LINE
Short: Success in the future
Long: Wealth and happiness
Ends in a star shape: Fame

6. LUCK LINE
Clear line: 30 years of luck
Gaps in line: Less-fortunate periods in life

7. RELATIONSHIP LINE
Long, horizontal line: One dominant, happy relationship
More than one line: Several relationships affect your life
Curves upward at the end: A successful relationship
Curves downward at the end: A difficult ending

8. TRAVEL LINES
The more you have, the greater your desire to travel.

9. INTUITIVE LINE
Having this line means you are impulsive.

THE COLORS OF A RAINBOW

Red • Orange • Yellow
Green • Blue • Indigo • Violet

──────UNDERPANTS THROUGH HISTORY──────

When the hidden tomb of the ancient Egyptian pharaoh Tutankhamen was discovered, 150 loincloth wrappings were found with him. Experts believe they are the early forerunners of today's underpants.

At the beginning of the 20th century, most people wore "all-in-ones," which combined underpants with a vest.

In the 1930s, separates became popular. Briefs swept the nation and the word *underpants* entered the dictionary. The world's first briefs were produced by Coopers Inc. The "Brief Style 101" was first available only to employees of the company but was launched publicly in 1935.

When briefs were first introduced, left-handed men were advised to wear them inside out.

"Days of the week" underpants were a craze in the 1950s. Each pair of underpants in the set of seven was labeled with a different day of the week.

Colorful underpants first hit stores in 1978.

In 1997, *The Adventures of Captain Underpants* was published, introducing a superhero who saves the world wearing just his underpants and a cape.

Whales and dolphins have an extra sense, called bio-magnetism, that they use to navigate. They find their way by detecting variations in Earth's magnetic field. Bees, frogs, and hamsters also have this extra sense.

THE DIATONIC SCALE

The white keys on a piano correspond to the diatonic scale of
C major (C-D-E-F-G-A-B-C), with the notes one whole tone
(or step) apart, except for E-F and B-C, which have an
interval of one semitone (half a tone).

In singing lessons, the diatonic scale is sometimes represented
by the scale "do-re-mi-fa-sol-la-ti-do."

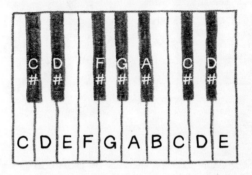

MIND READER

1. Ask a friend to think of a number between two and nine.

2. Ask them to multiply that number by nine.

3. Ask them to add the two digits of the result and then
   subtract five.

4. Tell your friend to think of the letter of the alphabet that
   corresponds to that number (1 is A, 2 is B, etc.)

5. Tell them to think of a country that starts with that letter.

6. Now tell them to pick the next letter of the alphabet and
   an animal that starts with that letter.

7. Now tell them you know what they are thinking, and that it
   is "Elephants in Denmark."

Most people will come up with this answer.

20TH-CENTURY TOYS

1900................................Plasticine
1902............................Teddy bear
1913.................Crossword puzzle
1921.............................Pogo stick
1943..............................Silly Putty
1946...................................Slinky
1948....................................Frisbee
1958............................Skateboard
1958....................................Legos
1975.........................Rubik's Cube
1996............................Tamagotchi

WORLD'S WORST SHIP DISASTERS

GENERAL SLOCUM
1904 • Caught fire • 900
killed, over 4,000 injured

RMS *TITANIC*
1912 • Hit an iceberg
• 1,503 killed

EMPRESS OF IRELAND
1914 • Collided in fog with
the *Storstad* • 1,078 killed

SS *LANCASTRIA*
1940 • Sunk by German
bombers• At least
2,000 killed

MS *ESTONIA*
1994 • Bow doors
failed • 852 killed

MV *WILHELM GUSTLOFF*
1945 • Torpedoed by
Russian submarine
• Over 7,000 killed

*HERALD OF FREE
ENTERPRISE*
1987 • Capsized • 193 killed

MV *DOÑA PAZ*
1986 • Collided with an
oil tanker • At least
2,900 killed

SS *MONT BLANC*
1917 • Collided with
steamship the *Imo.* Cargo of
explosives caught fire
• Over 2,000 killed

TONGUE TWISTERS

"Peter Piper picked a peck of pickled peppers.
A peck of pickled peppers Peter Piper picked.
If Peter Piper picked a peck of pickled peppers,
where's the peck of pickled peppers Peter Piper picked?"

"How much wood would a woodchuck chuck
if a woodchuck could chuck wood?
He would chuck, he would, as much as he could,
and chuck as much wood as a woodchuck would
if a woodchuck could chuck wood."

"She sells sea shells by the seashore."

"Sam's shop stocks short spotted socks."

"A noisy noise annoys an oyster."

"Just think, that sphinx has a sphincter that stinks!"

"Six slippery snails slid slowly seaward."

"Which witch wished which wicked wish?"

"Many an anemone sees an enemy anemone."

THE ROSWELL INCIDENT

Farmer Mac Brazel was walking in his fields near Roswell, New Mexico, on July 3, 1947, when he came across some silver wreckage made of an unusual, strong, springy material. Grady Barnett, an engineer, was a short distance away. He found in the wreckage a disk-shaped object and the bodies of several hairless creatures with large heads. Officials from the Roswell Army Air Field arrived at the scene and ordered everyone to leave. An announcement was made later that the wreckage belonged to a crashed weather balloon, and reporters were shown the remains of such a balloon. Mac Brazel claimed this was not the same material that he had found. He stated that what he had seen was "like nothing of this Earth." Major Jesse Marcel, an Army Air Forces intelligence officer, later admitted to taking part in a cover-up.

PERFECT PAINTING?

In 1961, it was discovered that *Le Bateau*, a painting by Henri Matisse, had been hanging upside down at New York's Museum of Modern Art for 46 days. Some 116,000 visitors had seen the picture, and not a single one had pointed out that anything was wrong.

THE LARGEST CITIES TODAY	THE LARGEST CITIES IN 1900
(BY POPULATION)	(BY POPULATION)
Tokyo, Japan 35,100,100	London, England 6,581,000
New York 8,085,000	New York 3,437,000
Mexico City, Mexico 20,950,000	Paris, France 2,714,000
São Paulo, Brazil 19,900,000	Berlin, Germany 1,889,000
Mumbai (Bombay), India 18,400,000	Chicago 1,699,000

————BURIAL CUSTOMS OF ANCIENT EGYPT————

A belief in immortality and physical resurrection was central to Egyptian religion. Egyptians believed that when all the elements that were present in life (soul, name, shadow, heart, and body) were reunited, the person would be resurrected.

The body had to be attractive enough to lure back the soul and other elements, and trained embalmers took great care to preserve it.

In the process of mummification, the brain, intestines, and other vital organs were removed, washed in palm wine, and placed in vases, known as canopic jars, filled with herbs. The body cavities were filled with powder of myrrh and other aromatic perfumes. The incisions were stitched, and the body was placed in niter (potassium nitrate) for 70 days, after which it was washed, wrapped in cotton bandages, dipped in a gummy substance, and finally put in a coffin and entombed.

In order to protect the valuable equipment of the dead from tomb robbers, the burial chambers were cut very deep into the ground and protected with stone portcullis blockings.

Ancient Egyptians believed all the objects that made life comfortable when alive should supply the same service in the afterlife. The dead were buried with supplies of food and drink, tools, weapons, garments, jewelry, and games. Servants were also expected to serve their dead masters, and would accompany them to their tombs, sealed in alive!

——————————SLEEP——————————

Ants never sleep.

Dolphins sleep with one eye open.

Horses can sleep standing.

Some birds can sleep while in flight.

A snail can sleep for three years.

HOW TO MAKE A PAPER AIRPLANE

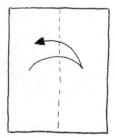

1. Take an 8½-inch-by 11-inch sheet of paper and crease it along the middle by folding it in half lengthwise.

2. Fold down the top corners inward to the center crease, making two right-angle triangles. Fold the large top triangle over and down.

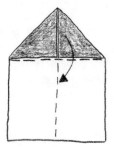

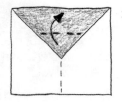

3. Fold the lower part of the tip of the large triangle up again, but not quite up to the top.

4. Fold and unfold the top corners inward to the center crease.

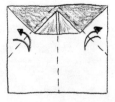

5. Now, bisect the new folds you made, using the previous creases as a guide. Fold and unfold along the two dashed lines.

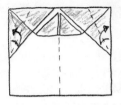

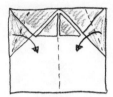

6. Now, fold the two large right-angle triangles down again.

7. Fold inward along the two dotted and dashed folds, tucking the triangles well underneath, snugly locking them in place.

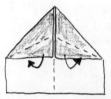

8. Now, make a few extra folds. Where you see the dotted and dashed lines in the diagram, fold these wings inward. Fold the small triangles outward to make winglets that help balance the plane in flight.

Top tip: This is a slow and graceful flyer. It flies best if you don't throw it hard, but simply release it as your hand moves forward a little.

---SINGING-VOICE RANGES---

CASTRATO

A castrato is a man who sings with a very high voice (equivalent to a soprano or mezzo-soprano), an effect produced by castration of the singer before puberty (i.e., removal of the boy's testicles). This practice began in the 16th century, when the Catholic Church in Europe had banned women from singing in choirs, and reached its peak in 17th- and 18th-century opera. The practice was not outlawed in Italy until 1870.

SOPRANO
Highest female voice

MEZZO-SOPRANO
Female voice between soprano and contralto

CONTRALTO
Lowest female voice

TREBLE
Highest (unbroken) male voice

COUNTERTENOR
Male voice, similar to tenor, but more frequently uses a higher range.

TENOR
High male voice

BARITONE
Male voice, lower than a tenor but higher than a bass

BASS
Lowest male voice

The song most frequently sung in the Western world is "Happy Birthday to You."

——BIRTHDAY TRADITIONS AROUND THE WORLD——

Being lifted up and down on a chair (Israel)

Eating noodles to promote your long life (China)

Flying flags outside your window (Denmark)

Greasing your nose with butter or margarine (Canada)

A pull on your earlobe for each year you've lived (Brazil)

A birthday pie with a greeting carved into its crust (Russia)

All birthdays are celebrated on New Year's Day (Vietnam)

A song and dance with a friend in front of your class
at school (Norway)

A mixture of rice yogurt and coloring wiped on your forehead
for good luck (Nepal)

———————————BLIND SPOT———————————

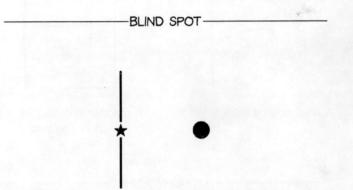

Cover your right eye and stare at the black dot.
Gradually move the page closer toward you. At a
certain distance the star will vanish, caused by the
"blind spot" on your optic nerve. The vertical line
will appear continuous, caused by your brain filling
in the missing information with a "guess."

DROODLES

Droodles are a cross between drawings and doodles.

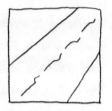

Street lines painted by
someone who had hiccups.

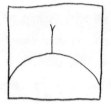

Almost-bald man with
a split end.

A chef hanging from a cliff.

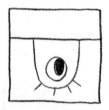

A monster checking for kids
under the bed.

MONDAY'S CHILD

Monday's child is fair of face,
Tuesday's child is full of grace,
Wednesday's child is full of woe,
Thursday's child has far to go,
Friday's child is loving and giving,
Saturday's child works hard for a living,
And the child that is born on the Sabbath day
is bonny and blithe, and good and gay.

─────MYSTERIOUS MONSTERS─────

BIGFOOT – Movie footage captured a large, hairy creature in a Californian forest. Some experts say it is a direct descendant of a kind of giant ape that once lived in China. Bigfoot is described as standing 7–10 ft. (2–3 m) tall and weighing over 500 lb. (225 kg), with footprints 17 in. (43 cm) long.

NESSIE – People have reported seeing a mysterious creature in Loch Ness, a lake in Scotland. Despite several alleged sightings, Nessie has never been found. The monster may be a sturgeon, a fish with a long snout and bony lumps on its back. Sturgeon can grow to 20 ft. (6 m) long.

STORSIE – People claim to have seen a sea monster in Lake Storsjön, Sweden. Some say the beast has a head like a horse; others say it's a big, wormlike serpent. Accounts agree that the creature has large eyes and an enormous mouth and is 30–40 ft. (9–12 m) in length.

MOKELE-MBEMBE – From the jungles of Africa have come many reported sightings of a strange beast known as Mokele-Mbembe. Described as an animal with a long neck and tail, and round-shaped feet with three claws, it has all the characteristics of a sauropod dinosaur!

YETI – A mysterious creature is said to live in the Himalayan Mountains of Asia. It is reported to be big, apelike, hairy, and smelly. Some people call it the Abominable Snowman; others call it Yeti, which means "big eater."

─────────────── HOW TO MAKE A VOLCANO ───────────────

You will need: a large work area (this can get pretty messy, so use newspaper or make your volcano in the garden), modeling clay (brown and red), baking soda, red food coloring, liquid dishwasher detergent, vinegar.

1. Make the outside of the volcano with modeling clay. Use brown clay for the base and red clay for the rim to make it look like red-hot lava.

2. Scoop out a hole at the top of the volcano and stir in 1 tablespoon of baking soda, a few drops of red food coloring and a few drops of liquid dishwasher detergent.

3. Pour in ¼ cup of vinegar, stand well back, and watch the volcano erupt!

─COUNTRIES WITH NUCLEAR-WEAPONS CAPABILTY─

England • China • France • Pakistan
India • Russia • United States • Israel

SEEKING TO OBTAIN
Iran • North Korea

ABANDONED
South Africa • Belarus • Kazakhstan • Ukraine

─────────────── CAN YOU HELP ME? ───────────────

Portuguese	"Pode-me ajudar?"
German	"Können Sie mir helfen?"
French	"Pouvez-vous m'aider?"
Italian	"Puoi aiutarmi?"
Turkish	"Yardim edebilir misiniz?"
Indonesian	"Boleh baypak tolong saya?"
Spanish	"Puede ayudarme?"

———— BODY LANGUAGE ————

Biting nails...Insecurity, nervousness

Lounging on chair with arms dangling...............................Relaxed

Standing with hands on hips.............................Readiness, aggression

Arms crossed on chest..Defensiveness

Touching or rubbing nose.....................................Rejection, lying

Rubbing eyes...Doubt

Locked ankles..Apprehension

Rubbing hands..Anticipation

Hands clasped behind head...........................Confidence, superiority

Open palm...Sincerity, openness

Pinching bridge of nose, eyes closed.....................................Foreboding

Tapping or drumming fingers.......................................Impatience

Patting/fondling hair...Insecurity

Tilted head...Interest

Stroking chin..Making a decision

Looking down, face turned away...................................Disbelief

Pulling or tugging at ear..Indecision

The oldest plants in the world are the macrozamia plants of Australia, which often live for 5,000 to 7,000 years and may even reach twice that age.

--- **HOW TO CHEAT** ---

Record all the answers onto a tape recorder and tell the teacher that you find it relaxing to listen to music through earphones • Write the answers on your sleeve • Paste the cover of your textbook over the study guide and take that in instead • Make friends with a kid from another school who takes the exam the day before • Phone a friend • Get someone to take the exam for you • Faint • Shout "Fire!" and sneak a peak at the other papers on your way out.

--- **Fs** ---

Count the number of Fs in the following sentence:

"Finished files are the result of years of scientific study combined with the experience of years."

Look at the answer only after you have counted them!

There are six. The brain doesn't process *of*. Anyone who counts all six Fs on the first go is a genius. Three is normal.

> Bulls don't charge when they see red. They are color-blind and are provoked by movement.

CONSTELLATIONS

Originally, a constellation was a distinct pattern of stars. In 1930, astronomers agreed to divide the sky into 88 areas, like countries on a map of Earth, each containing a different constellation. The constellation name can now refer to this area of sky as well as the star pattern it contains. The star patterns rarely look exactly like their names suggest, but are a helpful way of grouping selections of stars.

Some constellation names date back thousands of years. Most were given their names by Greek astronomers and refer to mythological creatures.

Ursa Major, the Great Bear, shows an unusual bear with a long tail, and also includes the well-known plow pattern.

Centaurus shows the creature from Greek myth who was half man, half horse. The constellation includes two bright stars, Alpha Centauri and Hadar. Of all bright stars, Alpha Centauri is the closest to Earth.

The smallest constellation is Crux Australis.

The largest constellation is Hydra, the Water Serpent.

MOST-INTELLIGENT ANIMALS

Human	Monkey
Chimpanzee	Whale
Gorilla	Dolphin
Orangutan	Elephant
Baboon	Pig
Gibbon	Parrot

The southern giant petrel, or "vulture of the Antartic," is extremely vicious and is often seen violently attacking penguins and tearing the flesh from dead seals and whales. Another name given to giant petrels is "stinker," due to their ability to spit blobs of oil and regurgitated food at their enemies.

—YOUNG ACHIEVERS—

Thomas Young (age 8) spoke 12 languages.

David Morgan (age 13) swam the English Channel.

Nadia Comaneci (age 14) received seven perfect scores for gymnastics in the Olympics.

Balamurali Ambati (age 17) became a doctor.

Benedict IX (age 12) became pope.

WHY DID THE CHICKEN CROSS THE ROAD?

To get to the other side.

To show the cow it could be done.

To stretch its legs.

To prove it wasn't chicken.

Because every time she did, people made a joke about it.

Don't ask me—ask the chicken.

Scre-e-e-e-ech! . . . THUMP! . . . We shall never know.

MOST NEIGHBORS

China is the country with the most neighbors. Along its borders are Afghanistan, Bhutan, India, Kazakhstan, Kyrgyzstan, Laos, Macau, Mongolia, Myanmar, Nepal, North Korea, Pakistan, Russia, Tajikistan, Uzbekistan, and Vietnam.

ANIMALS USED IN WAR

PARROTS
In World War I, parrots were perched on the Eiffel Tower, from where they could give 20 minutes' warning of approaching aircraft.

BATS
In World War II, the U.S. army was preparing to strap napalm to the backs of bats and then release them over Japan. An accident during trials destroyed a general's car, and the plan was abandoned.

DOLPHINS
Dolphins were used by the U.S. army to detect enemy mines during the war in Iraq in 2003.

ELEPHANTS
The Carthaginians first used elephants against Rome at the siege of Agrigentum in 262 BC.

DOGS
In World War II, Russian soldiers strapped bombs to dogs to destroy German tanks.

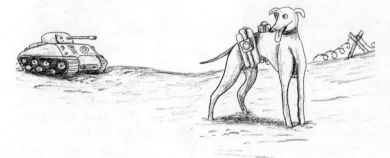

SICK AS A PARROT

The term comes from the parrot disease psittacosis. The disease was not that harmful to birds but could easily be transmitted to humans and often resulted in death. It was particularly rife aboard pirate ships. Symptoms included fever, dry cough, and severe muscle pain. Psittacosis was caught from inhaling the dust of dried parrot poo.

SKATEBOARDING TRICKS

DROP-IN
Entering a ramp

FLIP TRIP
Spinning the board

KICK FLIP
An air trick—flicking the
heel side of the board
with your front foot,
spinning the board, then
landing back on it

AIR
When all four wheels
are in the air

CARVE
Turning with all wheels
on the ground

BAIL
Jumping off the board
to avoid injury

OLLIE
Smacking the tail of the
board on the ground with
your back foot while your
front foot pulls the board
into the air

NOLLIE
A nose ollie, using the front
foot to smack the board
against the ground

TWEAK
Twisting your body with
the board

FAKIE
Riding backward

MANUAL
Cruising on the back wheels

JUDO
An air trick—grabbing
the heel edge of the board
with your front hand and
kicking the front foot out

BACKSLIDE
Turning in the direction
your toes point

GRIND
Sliding the board along an
obstacle, like a curb

GYRATE
Pumping the board
to gain speed

INDY GRAB
An air trick—grabbing
the toe edge of the board
with your back hand and
poking the nose out

HEEL FLIP
An air trick—flicking the
toe side of the board
with the ball of the
front foot

TAIL SLIDE
Sliding the underside of
the tail on a ledge or
lip of an obstacle

────────WHO IS YOUR TRUE LOVE?────────

Twist the stem of an apple and recite the alphabet until the stem comes off—the last letter you said is the first initial of your true love. Tap the tough end of the stem against the skin of the apple and recite the alphabet until the skin breaks—the last letter you said is the last initial of your true love.

Honey is the only food that does not spoil. Honey from jars found in the tombs of Egyptian pharaohs has been tasted by archaeologists and found to be edible.

────────HISTORICAL JOBS FOR CHILDREN────────

WATERBOYS
Brought water to construction workers.

OFFICE BOYS
Worked in offices sharpening pencils, stuffing envelopes, sweeping floors, and running errands.

GILLIE BOYS
Worked on boats helping fishermen bait hooks, pull nets, and prepare food.

POWDER MONKEYS
Carried gunpowder to ships' cannons during battle.

CHIMNEY SWEEPS
Were sent up chimneys to loosen soot.

VENDORS
Sold food and drink on city streets.

LOBLOLLIES
Worked on naval ships as surgeons' assistants.

EGG-STRAORDINARY

Of all birds, the kiwi lays the largest egg in proportion to its body size, sometimes weighing more than a quarter of its body weight.

An ostrich egg is 24 times larger than a hen's egg. It takes 42 minutes to boil and 80 minutes to hard boil, and a man can stand on the shell without it cracking.

Add sugar to a glass of water, then put an egg into the water. The egg will float.

The incubation temperature of turtle and tortoise eggs directly influences the sex of the hatchling.

The female egg cell is the largest of all cells in the human body.

WHO'S AFRAID OF DENTISTS?

The first dentists in Japan perfected special finger exercises so they could pull teeth with their bare hands.

Tooth drawers in ancient China used to spend hours pulling out nails hammered into planks of wood as practice for extracting teeth with their fingers.

The first dentist's drill was driven by a wheel. It tended to vary in speed and sometimes stopped mid-operation.

It wasn't until 1872 that the first efficient rotary dental drill was introduced.

CITIES BY ANOTHER NAME

Chicago..The Windy City

Edinburgh, Scotland............................The Athens of the North

Jerusalem, Israel....................................The City of David

London, England...The Smoke

Los Angeles......................................The City of Angels

New York...The Big Apple

Paris, France...The City of Light

Rome, Italy...The Eternal City

St. Petersburg, Russia.........................The Venice of the North

Venice, Italy....................................The Bride of the Sea

WHAT'S THE USE?

Silent alarm clock

Double-sided playing cards

Inflatable anchor

Smooth sandpaper

Nonstick sticky tape

Waterproof sponge

Fireproof matches

Glow-in-the-dark sunglasses

Inflatable dart board

Helicopter ejector seat

WATER BET

1. Put a glass of water on a table and then put a hat over it.

2. Tell your friend you can drink the water without touching the hat.

3. Go under the table and make drinking sounds.

4. Get up, and act as though you've drunk the water.

5. When your friend lifts the hat to check, pick up the glass of water and drink it.

Now you've drunk the glass of water without touching the hat!

CURIOUS CURES

WOUNDS and ACHES
Wipe drops of human tears
over the afflicted area.

MUMPS
Walk around a pigsty
three times.

EPILEPSY
Bathe in the blood
of a gladiator.

PLAGUE
Get breathed on
by a billy goat.

DIABETES
Eat dried and
powdered mice.

RHEUMATISM
Carry a strangely shaped
potato around with you.

WHOOPING COUGH
Eat baked mice
with onions.

JAUNDICE
Swallow a live spider
rolled in butter.

PARENTS ALWAYS SPEAK THE TRUTH

"If you eat your crusts, your hair will go curly."

"Eating greens will help grow hair on your chest."

"If you pull an ugly face and the wind changes,
you will stay like that."

"If you swallow chewing gum, it will stay inside you
forever."

"If you swallow an apple seed, an apple tree will
grow inside you."

TYPES OF GHOSTS

WILL-O'-THE-WISPS
Spirits or imps appearing
as faint green and red lights
seen at night, trying to lead
travelers to danger.

BANSHEES
Ghosts of young women
who wail at night in forests,
warning of danger and
impending death.

PSYCHIC IMPRINTS
Ghosts that are the result
of emotions left in a place,
and that play out the events
that occurred there.

GHOST VEHICLES
Vehicles that suddenly
appear on the road
traveling at high speeds,
only to disappear.

POLTERGEISTS
Means "noisy ghosts," and
thus any phenomenon
involving sounds, the
movement of objects, or
physical assaults made by
an unseen force.

GUARDIANS
Ghosts or spirits of
deceased loved ones
who appear to the living
to offer guidance or
protection.

DOPPELGÄNGERS
Spirits roaming freely
in the world as
physical copies of
living people. If you
meet up with your
doppelgänger, your death
will soon follow.

ORGANIZED RELIGIONS

RELIGION	HOLY WRITING
Christianity	Bible
Islam	Koran
Hinduism	Vedas
Buddhism	Dharma
Sikhism	Guru Granth Sahib
Judaism	Torah

INSPECTOR GADGET'S BEST GADGETS

Hilarious gas
Squirt gun
Copter
Rocket skates
Binoculars
Umbrella
Lasso
Satellite dish (super hearing)

Springs (hat and shoe)
Top-secret phone
Skeleton key
Cuckoo clock
Boxing glove
Can opener
Claw bumper
Rear ejection seat

THE BLACK DEATH

The Black Death killed about a third of the population of the Middle East and Europe in the mid-14th century. It was a form of bubonic plague and took its name from swellings of blood that formed under the victim's skin and turned black. The plague was carried by rat fleas that could also live on humans.

The dead were piled into burial pits until they overflowed. Also, bodies (and sometimes living victims) were shut in houses that were then burned to the ground.

A WEEK WITH THE BLACK DEATH

Day one...Headaches, chills, and fever
Day two...Nausea, vomiting
Day three...Soreness in arms and legs
Day four...Swellings appear on neck and limbs
Day five......................Swellings split open and ooze pus and blood
Day six...Internal bleeding
Day seven...Death

HOW TO DRIBBLE A BASKETBALL

You are not allowed to run
with the ball, so dribbling is a
crucial skill. You may use only
one hand at a time, and, once
you have stopped dribbling,
you must pass or shoot.

1. Gain control of the ball
   by spreading your fingers
   over its top.

2. Begin the dribble by pushing
   the ball firmly to the floor.
   Use your hand and wrist to
   control the height and
   speed of the bounce.

3. Keep your hand on top of the ball so that it rebounds
   accurately, and keep the bounce height to waist level. Try
   not to let the ball hit the palm of your hand. Feel the ball
   with your fingers and let your wrists do the work.

4. Move forward on the balls of your feet and bend your
   knees to maintain your balance.

   Top tips: Keep your body over the ball to shield the ball
   from your opponents. To help keep possession, dribble
   with the hand farther away from your opponent.

Wadakin and Matsuzaka beef, from Japan, are
considered to be the two most tender kinds of
beef in the world. The cattle from which this meat
is taken are isolated in dark stalls, fed on beer
and beer mash, and hand massaged three times
a day by specially trained beef masseurs.

---MAZES OF THE WORLD---

Roman maze

Medieval maze at
Chartres, France

Ancient Greek maze
from Crete

Hampton Court maze in
London, England—the oldest
permanent hedge maze
in the world

LOST IN A MAZE

A unicursal maze has only one path to follow, and
while it may feel like you are getting lost as you
twist and turn, you will eventually reach the goal.

A multicursal maze has branches and forks that
require you to guess the correct path.

If lost, apply the "right-hand rule." Keep your right
hand against the maze wall as you walk. You are
guaranteed a way out.

───────MYTHICAL CREATURES───────

Centaur..Half man, half horse

Cerberus.............................Three-headed hound with a snake's tail

Chimera.........Goat's body with a lion's head and a serpent's tail

Cyclops..Giant with one eye in its forehead

Echidna...Half woman, half serpent

Gorgon.........................Each of three sisters with serpents for hair

Harpy.............Face of an old hag, body of a bird with long claws

Minotaur...Half man, half bull

Pegasus...Winged horse

Phoenix.............Bird that lives 500 years, burns itself on a funeral pyre, and rises, reborn, from the ashes

Satyr.....................Man with goat's legs and hooves and pointy ears

Unicorn...............................Horse with a single horn on its forehead

──────────JUMP-ROPE RHYME──────────

Two people turn the rope and chant the rhyme.
Three jumpers jump in and perform the actions.

I had a little puppy
His name was Tiny Tim
I put him in the bathtub, to see if he could swim.
He drank up all the water. He ate a bar of soap.
The next thing I knew, he had a bubble in his throat.
In came the doctor. *(Person one jump in)*
In came the nurse. *(Person two jump in)*
In came the lady with the alligator purse.
(Person three jump in)
Out went the doctor. *(Person one jump out)*
Out went the nurse. *(Person two jump out)*
Out went the lady with the alligator purse.
(Person three jump out)

--- TO MAKE A WISH ---

See three birds on
a telephone wire.

Blow out the candles on
your birthday cake.

Throw an eyelash over
your left shoulder.

Eat a green M&M.

Snap a wishbone.

See a falling star.

Burn onions.

See a robin in spring.

Throw a coin in a well.

--- TORNADOES ---

A tornado is a vortex of violently rotating winds that
looks like funnel-shaped clouds.

On May 3, 1999, scientists recorded a tornado with
a wind speed of 302 mph (486 kph), the fastest
ever, in Oklahoma.

The record number of tornadoes over a 24-hour period
is 148. They took place at Tornado Alley, in the Midwest,
April 3-4, 1974.

--- HIGHEST LIFE EXPECTANCY ---

Andorra..............85.5 years	Sweden.................80.1 years
San Marino..........81.5 years	Switzerland..........80.1 years
Japan.....................81.1 years	Canada...............79.9 years
Singapore..........80.5 years	Iceland.................79.9 years
Australia.............80.2 years	Italy.......................79.4 years

FIRST AID

ELECTRIC SHOCKS
During electrocution, a person may become stuck to what they are touching. Do not touch the person, or you will receive a shock as well. Turn the electricity off at the source. If this is not possible, push the person clear with a piece of wood. Be careful when moving someone who has been shocked. Their muscles will be weakened, and their bones are liable to break.

BURNS
If a person's clothing is on fire, roll them in a rug, blanket, or piece of carpet. This will stop air getting to the flames and put out the fire. Do not break blisters. If a person is scalded by hot water, remove tight-fitting clothes. For mild burns, keep the area in cold water or hold it under a cold running tap for ten minutes. Put medicinal cream only on sunburned skin.

EPILEPTIC FITS
If someone is having a fit, don't restrict their movement. Loosen their clothing and put something soft under their neck. Do not attempt to put anything in their mouth. When the fit is over, give the person time to be still and recover.

FAINTING
Fainting is caused by a lack of oxygen in the blood supplied to the brain. Loosen tight clothing, give the patient space to breathe, and open the windows if the room is hot or smoky.

Toenails should always be cut straight across, rather than following the shape of the toe. This prevents ingrown toenails.

FIRST TASTED

Hamburger	1836
Potato chips	1853
Chewing gum	1872
Coca-Cola	1886
Pop Tarts	1964

HOW TO DO AN OLLIE

The Ollie, invented in 1978 by Alan "Ollie" Gelfand, is the basis for most other skateboarding tricks. Without it, you can't jump onto or over obstacles.

1. As you skate, put your back foot on the tail of the board and your front foot midway between the nose and the tail.

2. Lower your center of gravity by crouching.

3. Push your back foot down on the tail of the board and straighten

   your legs, effectively jumping in the air. The downward force on the tail will make the board bounce upward.

4. As the board rises, drag your front foot to the nose of the board. When your foot is at the nose, press it down.

5. Lift your back foot to allow the tail to rise. The board will now be level as you reach the peak of the jump.

6. As you land, bend your knees and pull them toward your chest, then follow your board back down to the ground.

   Top tip: Remember to wear safety gear.

> When Sir Walter Raleigh was beheaded, his wife had his head embalmed. She carried it around with her until her own death 29 years later.

———————— THE ORIGINS OF WORDS ————————

TOAST – The term, used to propose good health before drinking, originated in Rome. A piece of spiced, burned bread was dropped into wine to improve the drink's flavor and absorb any sediment at the bottom of the glass.

DECIMATE – "To kill, destroy, or remove a large proportion of something," from the Latin *decimus* (tenth). Originally, the word referred to a Roman military tradition in which an entire body of troops would be punished for disobedience by decimation— that is, by the killing of every tenth man.

BEDLAM – A corruption of the name Bethlehem. The modern sense, meaning madness or confusion, takes its name from a famous insane asylum, the Hospital of Saint Mary of Bethlehem, London, England.

NIGHTMARE – A mare, from the Old English *maere*, was a demon, known as an incubus (male) or succubus (female), which visited you at night and caused you to have awfully frightening dreams.

BOUDOIR – Literally "a place to sulk in," derived from the French word *bouder*, meaning "to sulk."

COMPANION – From the French *compaignon*, ultimately from the Latin *companionem,* which translates as "one with whom you would eat bread," from *com* ("together with") and *panis*, ('bread").

GROGGY – From the description of the feeling that many British sailors experienced when they drank too much grog, a mixture of rum and water. Grog is said to have taken its name from the nickname "Old Grog," given to a British admiral by his sailors in 1740. He used to wear a kind of heavy coat of grogram, a coarse, weatherproof fabric. The sailors started to use their nickname for him when he reduced their weekly rations of rum by diluting it with water.

——————— LONGEST-REIGNING RULERS ———————

King Louis XIV (France)	72 years (1643–1715)
King John II (Liechtenstein)	71 years (1858–1929)
Emperor Franz Joseph (Austria-Hungary)	68 years (1848–1916)
Queen Victoria (England)	64 years (1837–1901)
Emperor Hirohito (Japan)	63 years (1926–1989)

———————————LEFT-HANDERS———————————

Most left-handers draw human figures facing to the right.

Over 1,500 left-handed people die every year in the world as a result of using products made for right-handed people.

Left-handers are commonly good at tennis, baseball, swimming, and fencing.

SOME LEFT-HANDED PEOPLE:

Mark Twain • Marilyn Monroe • Wolfgang Amadeus Mozart
Isaac Newton • Bart Simpson • Ludwig van Beethoven
Albert Einstein • Charlie Chaplin • Benjamin Franklin

Leonardo da Vinci could simultaneously draw with one hand and write with the other.

—————————WHAT DO YOU CALL A . . .?—————————

Boy at a door...Matt

Boy behind a bush...Russell

Girl with one leg...Eileen

Girl with a frog on her head.....................................Lily

Boy with cat scratches..Claude

Boy lost at sea...Bob

Boy who can't stand..Neil

Boy with a rabbit on his head....................Warren

Boy with a car on his head...............................Jack

Boy with a seagull on his head........................Cliff

Boy in a hole in the ground............................Doug

Boy with a toilet on his head...........................Lou

Girl with two toilets on her head......................Lulu

Girl in a vase..Rose

<table>
<tr><td colspan="2">—HOW LONG 'TIL—
I'M BORN?</td></tr>
</table>

—HOW LONG 'TIL—
I'M BORN?

Elephant calf	616 days
Rhinoceros calf	560 days
Horse foal	336 days
Cow calf	264 days
Human child	252 days
Grizzly-bear cub	210 days
Lion cub	119 days
Wolf pup	63 days
Badger kit	56 days
Cat kitten	48 days
Rabbit kitten	28 days
Squirrel pup	25 days

—ENDANGERED—
ANIMALS

Javan rhinoceros

Kakapo parrot

Pampas deer

Monk seal

Siberian tiger

Mountain gorilla

Asian elephant

Blue whale

Yangtze River dolphin

Giant panda

Salmon

Jaguar

———HOW TO SURVIVE A VOLCANIC ERUPTION———

Make an evacuation plan so that everyone in your family knows where to go if you need to leave.

Prepare provisions. Stock up early on water, food, blankets, and medical supplies. Be sure to include disposable breathing masks and goggles.

Be aware of the hazards that can come with an eruption— flying debris, hot gases, lava flows, and the potential for explosions, mudslides, and avalanches.

Seek shelter in the event of a volcanic eruption. Close all doors and windows to prevent ash and debris from entering the house.

Collect water in your bathtubs, sinks, and containers as soon as possible, as supplies may quickly become polluted.

———————HOW MANY SIDES?———————

3	triangle	9	nonagon	15	pentadecagon
4	quadrilateral	10	decagon	16	hexadecagon
5	pentagon	11	hendecagon	17	heptadecagon
6	hexagon	12	dodecagon	18	octadecagon
7	heptagon	13	tridecagon	19	enneadecagon
8	octagon	14	tetradecagon	20	icosagon

Llanfairpwllgwyngyllgogerychwyrndrobwllllantysiliogogogoch is the Welsh name of the town of Llanfair, in Wales. At the Llanfair railroad station, a 20-foot-long sign makes this clear to all arrivals. Translated, the name means "the church of Saint Mary in the hollow of the white hazel trees near the rapid whirlpool by St Tysilio's of the red cave."

SPIDER BITES

TARANTULA
Swelling, achiness

WHITE-TAILED SPIDER
Blisters, lesions, faintness

FUNNEL-WEB SPIDER
Cramps, rigidity, paralysis

BANANA SPIDER
Immediate pain, cold
sweats, possible death

VIOLIN SPIDER
Skin blisters, ulcers,
necrosis (tissue death)

SAC SPIDER
Pain two to eight hours after
being bitten, swelling,
possible scarring

WOLF SPIDER
Pain, itchiness,
dizziness, nausea

On average, a person will eat six spiders
in their lifetime, usually while asleep.

MOST-COMMON ALLERGENS

FOOD

Nuts

Cheese

Wheat

Seafood

ENVIRONMENT

Pollen

Molds

House-dust mites

Cats

——I DIDN'T DO MY HOMEWORK BECAUSE . . .——

"I have a solar-powered calculator and the sun went down."

"I must need glasses. I really couldn't see myself doing it."

"My family got a new paper shredder and we had to see if it was working."

"Homework? I was supposed to bring that to school? I thought it stayed at home."

"You asked me to do it, but you didn't tell me to do it. I thought it was optional."

"My sister ate it."

"I left it in my shirt, and my mom put it in the washing machine."

"I forgot to take my dog for a walk, and he peed on it."

————————HOW MANY LEGS?————————

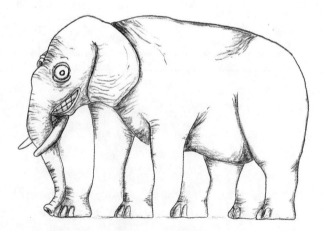

SPECIAL EFFECTS THAT CAN BE SEEN FROM EARTH

Aurora borealis (northern lights) • Meteor shower
Eclipse of the Sun • Lunar eclipse • Halo around the Moon

AURORAS

Colored glows called auroras are common around Earth's polar regions. They are caused by streams of particles from the Sun that are attracted by the magnetic poles. As the particles hit Earth's atmosphere, they cause atoms of gas to glow. Auroras can look like huge curtains hanging in the sky, slowly changing shape.

THE SPEED OF LIGHT

The galaxy is so large that light takes 100,000 years to travel fully across it. Light travels at approximately 186,000 miles a second. To look at the farthest visible star, you are looking four billion years into the past. The light from the star has taken that many years to reach you!

THE ECLIPTIC

The Sun moves along a path in the sky known as the ecliptic. The path of the Moon and the planets lie close to the ecliptic.

The constellations around the ecliptic are known as the Zodiac, a name that comes ultimately from a Greek word for "animal."

ANIMALS LAUNCHED INTO SPACE

Dogs • Mice • Chimpanzees • Cats
Spiders • Jellyfish • Insects

CROOKED CARDS

A great card trick with a crooked tale that is guaranteed to baffle your friends!

Before performing the trick, take four random cards. Remove the four jacks from the pack and place them underneath the four random cards.

Take the bundle of eight cards tightly in your hand, and show your audience the jack on the bottom, saying, "Here are four robbers (the jacks), and they are going to rob the bank (the deck of cards)."

Then say, "The four robbers landed on top of the bank in a helicopter." (Place the stack of cards on top of the deck.)

Next say, "The first robber goes to the first floor." (Move the top card to the bottom.)

Then say, "The second robber goes to the second floor." (Move the next card close to the bottom.)

Then say, "The third robber goes to the third floor." (Move the next card closer to the top.)

Then say, "The fourth robber goes to the stairs of the fourth floor." (Move this card just underneath the four jacks.)

Now the audience thinks you have moved all the jacks into the deck, but you have actually moved the four random cards.

Then say, "The police arrived, and, one by one, the robbers rushed upstairs to escape."

Show your audience the four jacks at the top!

CAN YOU . . . ?

Curl your tongue • Do a belly roll
Wiggle your ears • Flip your eyelids
Touch your nose with your tongue
Rub your tummy and your head at the same time

FAMOUS FREAK-SHOW ATTRACTIONS

John Merrick
(The Elephant Man)

Grace McDaniels
(The Mule-faced Woman)

Chang and Eng
(The Siamese Twins)

Jo-Jo
(The Dog-faced Boy)

Julia Pastrana
(The Bearded Lady)

Frank Lentini
(The Three-legged Man)

Sealo
(The Seal Boy)

Susi
(The Elephant-skin Girl)

UNCOMMON PHOBIAS

Bogeys...Bogeyphobia

Beards..Pogonophobia

Phobias...Phobophobia

Old people...Gerontophobia

Dirt or germs..Mysophobia

School..Scolionophobia

Teenagers..Ephebiphobia

Vegetables...Lachanophobia

Sitting down...Kathisophobia

Long words...............Hippopotamonstrosesquipedaliophobia

Millions of trees are accidentally planted by squirrels who bury nuts and then forget where they hid them.

IN CASE OF FIRE

FIRE AT HOME

If you wake and smell smoke, get dressed before opening your bedroom door. Put on your shoes, wrap a blanket around you, and tie a handkerchief or towel around your head and mouth. Leave the room on hands and knees, as the air close to the floor is most free from smoke.

FIRE AT SCHOOL OR IN A PUBLIC BUILDING

In a school or public building, there is not only the danger of being burned but also the risk of being crushed or trampled when the crowd rushes to get through the main doors. When panic occurs and people hustle and press toward the door, look for another way of escape such as a back door or a window. If in the middle of a panic-stricken crowd, keep your head up, arms doubled up in front of your chest and your elbows at your sides. This gives you the best chance to breathe and resist pressure on your ribs.

MOST-COMMON LITTER

Chewing gum • Newspaper
Plastic bags • Cigarette ends
Candy wrappers • Matches
Glass fragments • Tinfoil

COLLECTORS

Philographist	Autographs
Bibliophile	Books
Numismatist	Coins
Plangonologist	Dolls
Copoclephile	Key rings
Deltiologist	Postcards
Conchologist	Shells
Philatelist	Stamps
Arctophile	Teddy bears
Lepidopterist	Butterflies
Vexillologist	Flags

───TRASH TO TREASURE───

Decorate cardboard tubes and old drink cartons
to make pencil holders.

Pick out your favorite pictures from old greeting cards
to make bookmarks and gift tags.

Recycle jars to make candleholders.

Use wallpaper or fabric to decorate books and storage boxes.

Use old clothes pegs to hold notes or photographs.

Decorate old CD cases to make freestanding picture frames.

Use old jeans or other fabric to make purses and secret
inside pockets for your clothes.

Howard Menger, from Virginia, announced
in 1956 that he was in touch with friendly
space people from Venus. He helped
disguise the Venusians to look like
humans, telling the men to cut their long,
blond hair. In return, he received moon
potatoes.

───DOG TALK───

HAPPY – Wags its tail from side to side, holds its head up, tongue hanging out.

SCARED – Drops its tail between its legs, flattens its ears, crouches down.

ANGRY – Tail raised over its back, bares its teeth and growls, hackles raised.

───CAT TALK───

HAPPY – Tail quivers, lies on its chest, eyes half closed, rolls over, paws up.

SCARED – Crouches down, flattens its ears, avoids direct eye contact.

ANGRY – Flicks its tail from side to side, arches its back, puffs up its fur.

─────────WHAT SCIENTISTS STUDY─────────

Herpetologist..Reptiles and amphibians
Entomologist...Insects
Lepidopterist...Butterflies and moths
Vulcanologist..Volcanoes
Coleopterist...Beetles
Agronomist..Soil and crops
Astronomer....................................The universe beyond Earth
Epidemiologist.......................................The spread of diseases
Ethnologist...Behavior patterns
Geneticist...How traits are inherited
Geologist......................................The physical history of Earth
Geographer...Earth's surface
Marine biologist...............................Ocean plants and animals
Meteorologist...................................Weather and climate
Paleontologist...Fossils
Seismologist..Earthquakes

─────────COUNT THE BLACK DOTS─────────

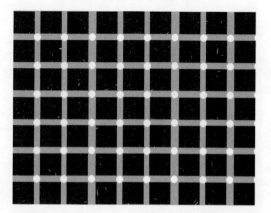

STUPID SIGNS

SHEEP, PLEASE KEEP DOGS UNDER CONTROL

No keyboard detected. Press any key to continue.

No muddy boots please or Dogs Smoking Ice cream

DUE TO PROBLEMS WITH LITTER, WE ASK ANYONE WITH RELATIVES BURIED IN THE GRAVEYARD TO DO THEIR BEST TO KEEP THEM IN ORDER

Be careful! Goats like to nibble your clothes and butt

TOILET OUT OF ORDER PLEASE USE FLOOR BELOW

———HOW TO PROTECT YOURSELF FROM A———
VAMPIRE IN THE MODERN WORLD

RINGING BELLS — Bells are known to drive away the undead. Try using a trilling ring tone on your mobile phone.

BLACK DOGS — Some believe black dogs are the enemies of vampires; others believe they may act as vampire assistants. Avoid them completely by getting your parents to buy you a ginger tabby or a gerbil instead.

KNOTS — Knotted string around doorways or on graves distracts vampires, because they allegedly feel compelled to untangle it. Hang your shoes from the knob of your bedroom door. The smell will also put them off, and they are more likely to try elsewhere, like your parents' room.

GARLIC — The classic vampire deterrent is a bulb of garlic worn around the neck or rubbed around doors or windows. Eating garlic bread and chicken Kiev may be just as effective.

HOLLY or JUNIPER — Keeping branches of certain trees in the house will deter vampires. Leave a branch on the floor for them to trip over in the dark.

SUNLIGHT — Vampires dissolve into dust as soon as a sunbeam hits them. If you can't wait till sunrise, try hitting them with your bedside lamp.

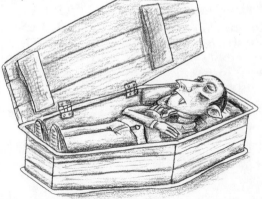

─────────HELLO, GOOD-BYE─────────

English	"Hello"	"Good-bye"
Italian	"Ciao"	"Arrivederci"
Russian	"Privet"	"Poka"
French	"Salut"	"Au revoir"
German	"Hallo"	"Auf Wiedersehen"
Greek	"Giásou"	"Andio sas"
Japanese	"Moshi Moshi"	"Ja, mata"
Portuguese	"Ola"	"Adeus"
Spanish	"Hola"	"Adiós"
Indonesian	"Hai"	"Selamat jalon"

─────TALLEST BUILDINGS IN THE WORLD─────

Taipei 101, Taiwan	1,667 ft. (508 m)
Petronas Towers, Malaysia	1,483 ft. (452 m)
Sears Tower, Chicago.	1,450 ft. (442 m)
Jin Mao Building, China	1,381 ft. (421 m)
Two International Finance Centre, Hong Kong	1,352 ft.(412 m)
CITIC Plaza, China	1,283 ft. (391 m)
Shun Hing Square, China	1,260 ft. (384m)
Empire State Building, New York	1,250 ft. (381 m)
Central Plaza, Hong Kong	1,227 ft. (374 m)

THE TALLEST STRUCTURE

The CN Tower, in Toronto, Canada, has been the world's tallest freestanding structure for nearly 30 years. It is 1,815 ft. (553.34 m) tall and features a glass floor at a height of 1,122 ft. (342 m), across which visitors can walk while looking straight down.

---------UNLUCKY 13---------

Many airports do not have a gate 13.

Hospitals and hotels often have no room number 13.

Italians do not have the number 13 in their national lottery.

Many American cities do not have a 13th Street or
a 13th Avenue.

On streets in Florence, Italy, the house between number 12
and 14 is addressed as 12 ½.

In France, people known as *quatorziens* ("fourteeners") were
employed to join dinner parties as a 14th guest.

It is considered bad luck to have 13 letters in your full name.

--------- WAYS TO PREDICT THE FUTURE ---------

Crystallomancy..Crystal balls

Foliomancy...Tea leaves

Oneiromancy..Dreams

Aeromancy.............Wind and atmospheric conditions

Ornithomancy.....................The flight patterns of birds

Bibliomancy...The Bible

Anthomancy..Flowers

Hippomancy.....................................Horse sounds

Ailuromancy...........................How a cat moves

Tiromancy...Cheese

--------- THE WORLD'S MOST-POPULAR FRUITS ---------

Bananas • Oranges • Grapes • Apples • Mangoes • Coconuts
Watermelons • Cantaloupes • Tangerines

————THE TRUTH BEHIND NURSERY RHYMES————

*Jack and Jill went up the hill
to fetch a pail of water
Jack fell down and broke his crown
And Jill came tumbling after.
Up got Jack, and home did trot
As fast as he could caper.
He went to bed and bound his head
With vinegar and brown paper.*

Jack and Jill are said to be King Louis XVI of France and Queen Marie Antoinette. The king was beheaded during the Reign of Terror in 1793, followed shortly by his queen (who came tumbling after).

*Mary Mary quite contrary
How does your garden grow?
With silver bells and cockleshells
And pretty maids all in a row.*

This rhyme is said to refer to the English queen Mary Tudor, or "Bloody Mary." She was a Catholic, and the garden in the rhyme refers to graveyards full of martyred Protestants who refused to give up their faith. The silver bells and cockleshells were instruments of torture, and the maids were devices for beheading people.

*Humpty Dumpty sat on a wall,
Humpty Dumpty had a great fall.
All the King's horses, and all the King's men
Couldn't put Humpty together again!*

Humpty Dumpty was a huge cannon used in the English Civil War (1642–49). The wall it sat on was damaged in cross fire, and Humpty Dumpty fell to the ground. The cannon was so heavy that the soldiers were unable to put it together again.

CURRENCIES

Australia	Dollar	Mongolia	Tugrik
Brazil	Real	the Netherlands	Euro
China	Yuan	Peru	Nuevo sol
Czech Republic	Koruna	Poland	Zloty
England	Pound sterling	Portugal	Euro
Ethiopia	Birr	Russia	Rouble
France	Euro	Saudi Arabia	Riyal
Germany	Euro	South Africa	Rand
Ghana	Cedi	South Korea	Won
Greece	Euro	Spain	Euro
India	Rupee	Sweden	Krona
Italy	Euro	Thailand	Baht
Japan	Yen	United States	Dollar
Malaysia	Ringgit	Venezuela	Bolivar
Mexico	Peso	Zambia	Kwacha

Until the 19th century, solid blocks of tea were used as money in Siberia.

Until the 20th century, dogs' teeth were used as money by natives of the Solomon Islands.

WHAT PARENTS REALLY MEAN

"We'll see." .... "No."

"Ask your father." .... "He can say no."

"Maybe when you're older." .... "Never."

"Do you think that's a good idea?" .... "Do you think I'm stupid?"

"Don't do anything I wouldn't do." .... "Don't do anything."

"We love you very much." .... "Please look after us when we are old and crazy."

YO-YO

The yo-yo is over 2,000 years old. It is thought to have originated in ancient Greece, where children played games with painted terra-cotta (clay) disks.

In the 1920s, the yo-yo was brought to the United States by Pedro Flores from the Philippines. His yo-yo was hand carved from a single piece of wood. It was unique because it was the first yo-yo that did not have the string tied to the axle. Instead, the string was looped around the axle, allowing the yo-yo to sleep, or spin, at the end of the string. Rather than being able to go only up and down, this yo-yo was capable of doing an infinite number of tricks.

HOW TO WALK THE DOG

With your yo-yo spinning quickly, gradually lower it until it just touches the floor.

Your yo-yo will start rolling forward along the floor. You are "walking the dog."

Jerk the yo-yo back to your hand before it stops spinning.

CALENDAR OF THE FUTURE

2009	Firefighting robots that can find and rescue people.
2010	Smart clothes that can alter their thermal properties.
2014	Robotic pets.
2014	First human landing on Mars.
2020	Cars that drive themselves on smart highways.
2025	Extension of average human life span to over 100 years.
2030	More robots than people in developing countries.
2035	Fully functioning artificial eyes and legs.

——————— **THE END** ———————

Finished

Closed

Over

Kaput

Done

Stopped

Time up

Start again